BODYBUILDING

The Hardgainers Guide to Building Muscle, Building Strength and Building Mass

Scrawny to Brawny
Skinny Guys Edition

AUGUSTUS SIMS

GET YOUR

FREE GIFT!

WAIT! – DO YOU LIKE FREE BOOKS?

My **FREE Gift** to You!! As a way to say **Thank You** for

downloading my book, I'd like to offer you more **FREE BOOKS!** Each time we release a NEW book, we offer it first to a small number of people as a test - drive. Because of your commitment here in downloading my book, I'd love for you to be a part of this group. You can join easily here → http://hardgainerguide.com/

Contents

Introduction 6

Chapter One   Why You're Not Gaining Muscle 9

Chapter Two   The Muscle Mindset...................................18

Chapter Three   Training for Real Muscle Mass..................22

Chapter Four   The Training Partner Factor.......................51

Chapter Five   Eating to Get Huge....................................61

Chapter Six   The Anabolic Advantage: 9 Ways to Get It....67

Chapter Seven   5 Super Supplements...................................95

Chapter Eight   Top 10 Muscle Building Shake Recipes ...110

Chapter Nine   Bringing It All Together...........................120

BONUS - Anabolic Recipes... 123

Conclusion 139

Introduction

Frustration.

Envy.

Exasperation.

If you're a hard-gainer then you've been through those emotions as you struggle in the gym for seemingly little reward. You see other guys who merely have to look at a weight to get pumped. Week by week they get bigger, stronger and more defined.

And then there's you.

You sweat. You strain. You push to failure, valiantly fighting for every ounce of new muscle. And still, the gains, if they do come, are painfully slow.

It's no wonder that you're just about ready to throw in the towel on this whole bodybuilding thing – and turn your attention to a less demanding endeavor, like cross-stitch!

Well, before you trade in your gym membership for a pair of knitting needles, take a look at this . . .

Like you, this guy was a hard gainer. In his teens he was skinny, lanky, picked on and depressed. When he picked up weights, the gains didn't come easily. Yet he persevered. Boy, did he persevere. On top of all of his limitations, this guy was nearly totally deaf. You may have heard of him.

His name's Lou Ferrigno.

There are thousands of hard gainer success stories. Not all of them have achieved the success of a Lou Ferrigno, but they have forged for themselves a muscular, strong body to be proud of. They've had to work harder than their gym peers – but that extra effort has made their achievements all the sweeter.

You can be among them.

You simply have to train – and eat – smarter to get there.

If you're a hard gainer, this manual is specifically designed for you. It will allow you stop spinning your wheels, getting you moving down the mass road, allowing you to consistently pack solid muscle onto your frame, build phenomenal strength and become the best built guy in the gym.

Chapter One

WHY YOU'RE
NOT GAINING MUSCLE

GENETICS

Building muscle is not an equal opportunity endeavor. Not everyone gains muscle at the same rate and not everybody has the talent to create the same level of development. Your individual genetics have a lot to do with how your body will respond to training.

Some people, like Arnold Schwarzenegger, started packing on pounds of solid muscle from the very beginning of their training career. Arnold touched his first weight at age 15, and was able to gain a half inch on his arms every couple of months.

Others who have become top level professional bodybuilders, like Frank Zane and Larry Scott, were the opposite to Arnold.

They had to fight and scratch for every ounce of muscle that they gained. Larry Scott, in fact, had the opposite shape to what you'd expect for bodybuilding - wide hips, narrow shoulder blades and skinny legs. Yet, he was able to build a physique that saw him crowned as the first ever Mr Olympia. His example, and that of countless others, reveals that bodybuilding is like the race between the hare and the tortoise. Ultimately, determination and endurance over a long period of time can win out over a quick start and sprint for the finish line.

Just as some people are naturally fast runners, or naturally good athletes, some people are naturally predisposed to building muscle. The following basic genetic factors come into play here:

- Testosterone levels - testosterone is the most important muscle building hormone in your body. Our genetics determine our natural levels.

- Muscle fiber distribution - people with a higher percentage of fast twitch muscle fibers are going to have grater muscle building potential. That's because fast twitch fibers are more prone to hypertrophy.

- Muscular shape - for the most part, there is very little you can do to influence the shape of an individual muscle.

Muscles can become bigger or smaller, but their actual shape in mostly predetermined by genetics.

• Recovery ability - some of us are able to tolerate more exercise than others. These people naturally have an advantage because they are able to successfully train and recover more often than others.

• Myostatin levels - the myostatin gene codes to limit the amount of muscle mass you can build. This gene will be more or less active depending on the individual.

The problem for hard gainers is that they don't get the immediate success, the positive feedback, that helps so much to keep a person motivated. In the long run, however, the satisfaction is that much greater, knowing that you have worked you ass for every ounce of muscle on your frame.

The real question for hard gainers, who are limited by their genetic potential, is *so what?*

Whatever you've been dealt with in the genetics department is what it is and can't be changed. All you can do is to make the very best of what you have and become the best YOU that you can possibly be. Whether you are able to gain muscle at an above average rate, at an average rate or at a below average rate is something that is set in stone and can't be changed. From a practical standpoint, it is absolutely irrelevant to your program.

It may not be possible to develop more rapidly than your biology will allow, but it is possible to develop more *slowly* than it will allow. Often this is because you do not truly believe that rapid gains are possible, and as a result, are not training as hard as you need to. Unless your goal is to become a world class bodybuilder - which is heavily dependent upon genetics - you CAN build an impressive, muscular body. By learning how to train hard, eat right and stay mentally zoned in, you will be able to pack real, solid mass onto your frame and double - even triple - your strength level, while getting lean and shredded.

RECOVERY

Muscle doesn't grow in the gym. In fact, your workouts are tearing your muscle down, quite literally. It is only when they are rested and fed, that they are able to bounce back to become bigger and stronger.

Most hard-gainers get into the mindset of more must be better. Their current training regime isn't producing the results they want, so they think that they have to train harder, do more and rest less in order to make the gains. That is a BIG mistake.

All successful muscle pumpers do just the opposite – rather than training more when they reach a sticking point, they a in order to allow their body to rest and recuperate.

A muscle is over-trained when it is trained so often that it doesn't get time to fully recover from the previous workout.

The body requires time to restore the chemical balance of the muscle cells, clear out the residual waste products, and restock the depleted stores of glycogen. But another factor is even more important: Time is needed for the cells themselves to adapt to the stimulus of the exercise and to grow. After all, bodybuilding is all about making muscles grow. So, if you over-train a muscle, forcing it to work too hard too quickly after the preceding exercise session, you will not give it a chance to grow and your progress will slow down.

Different muscles recover from exercise at different rates. The biceps recover the fastest. The lower back muscles recover the slowest, taking about a hundred hours to completely recuperate from a heavy workout. However, in most cases, giving a body part 48 hours' rest is sufficient, which means skipping a day after training a muscle before training it again.

Basic training involves only medium levels of intensity, so the time necessary for recovery is shorter. The harder you train, the higher the level of intensity. Another important factor is that trained muscles recover faster than untrained muscles. So the more adept you become at bodybuilding, the faster your recovery rate will be and the more intense your training can become.

FOOD

Most people don't appreciate how much food you need to eat to gain pure muscle mass. Eating may sound like a lot of fun, but consistently getting the basic ingredients of muscle building nutrition into your system in the amounts that will make a difference is challenging, to say the least. Unless, you provide your body with the building blocks of muscle food, you will never build a quality physique.

There are three basic nutrients that you need to build muscle and lose fat:

Protein: Protein, composed of various amino acids, provides the building blocks for muscle tissue. It is also a compound of all organs, and is involved in the structure of skin, bones, and tendons as well as being involved in many bodily functions.

Carbohydrates: Carbs provide fuel for energy, and are, in fact, the body's primary and most easily available source of energy. All carbs are sugar, molecules containing carbon, hydrogen, and oxygen, and oxygen synthesized by plants through the process of photosynthesis, using the energy from the sun, or by animals through the process of glycogen synthesis.

Fats: Fats are the most energy dense of the three macronutrients. Fats, which can be found in both plants and animals, are insoluble in water. Fat is the most calories dense of any nutrient. A pound of fat contains about 4,000 calories, as opposed to 1,800 calories stored in a pound of protein or carbohydrate.

TRAINING

If you're a hard-gainer, then you have probably tried every training program that is out there. Most of them have likely done very little for you. The reason could well be that the foundational theory upon which they have all been based is wrong. It is wrong for the average trainer but it is doubly wrong for the hard-gainer. That theory maintains that in order to get bigger muscles you have got to life heavier weight. In other words, to get big you must first get strong.

A lot of people believe that if they train to get strong, then they will build the physique that they want in the process. For the vast majority of people, though, this is like putting the cart before the horse. You should train for muscular development first, and the strength will come as a result of the development.

The misguided nature of people's thinking when it comes to building muscle is reflected in the age old question that bodybuilders get asked, "How much can you bench?" This question pre-supposes that a person's one rep maximum has something to do with the quality of their physique. Yet, one rep max strength has no place in a bodybuilding program.

Too many guys are obsessed with the weight on the bar. As a result they use sloppier and sloppier form. They end up training so as to recruit other muscle groups to help the target muscle to lift the weight. This is the opposite to what effective training does – isolate the working muscle group. For instance, a guy might load up the weight on a barbell curl to such an extent that they have to swing their lower back, thrust from the hips and throw their whole body into the lift. The biceps end up doing very little work.

Remember that the muscle cannot see how much weight is on the bar. All it knows is how hard it is being worked. The weight, then, should never be the end in itself. It should simply be a tool that is used to work the muscle. Increasing the weight is only one way to work the muscle harder and, as we shall discover, it is not the most efficient.

Rather than focusing on how much weight is being lifted, your attention needs to be directed to how much stress the working muscle is under. The key is not how much you can lift, but how hard you can work the muscle. Unlike a power-lifter or a weight lifter, your goal is not to simply move the weight from Point A to Point B. Your goal is to use the tool that is the weight to maximally work the muscle through it's full range of motion.

Chapter Two

THE MUSCLE MINDSET

You don't want to be one of those people who just goes through the motions in the gym. They are wasting their time. Rather, take a leaf out of the book of professional athletes who treat their workouts like a battlefield mission. If you want to get the most out of your training effort, you need to apply laser like focus to every aspect of your workout. In fact, you should divide your mental training focus into 2 aspects:

Before the Workout

During the Workout

BEFORE THE WORKOUT

(1) Mentally rehearse the workout in the hour before you hit the gym. See yourself grabbing the weights and powering through those last 3 difficult reps. Focus on your immediate goal, which is to do more than you did in your last workout - an extra rep, another 2 pounds of weight or a reduced rest between sets. Do this for every exercise.

(2) Discuss your specific workout plans for that day with your

buddies. Tell them you are absolutely focused on getting 8 reps with 30 pound dumbbells on the bench press. Put it out there.

(3) Surround yourself with positive people. Remember . . .

If you lay with dogs, you'll get up with fleas.

Actively seek out people who will support you. They will pull you

up when you need it and reinforce your daily **goals.**

(4) Be distracted early. When you first walk into the gym, pause

to take in the surroundings. Check out who's there and what's different. Doing this early allows you not to be distracted when you flick the switch and your workout begins.

(5) Build up your inner drive. An hour before your workout, your engine should be idling at a 4. By the time you walk into the gym it should be up to a 7. During your warm-up, it's reached 8.5. And by the time you pile the weight on for your first set, you're hitting 10.

DURING THE WORKOUT

(1) Focus directly on the working muscle group. Get connected. If you are doing barbell curls, put your mind into your biceps. Let nothing else matter. That way you'll be able to fully engage a muscle and recruit as many muscle fibers as possible.

(2) Switch off your brain. At least the part of it that is bent on

sabotaging your workout. You know the part. It's constantly trying to rationalize with you to get you to do less. So you don't injure yourself. So you don't run out of time. So you don't over-train. Don't negotiate with this side of your brain. Instead, tell your brain that what you're doing is easy. Don't focus on the weight that you're lifting. Visualize your body as a machine, your arms and legs as pistons, mechanically driving the weight up and down.

(3) Play mind games on yourself. This is a technique that professional athletes have been using for decades to produce almost superhuman results from their work-outs. Tom Platz is a legend among bodybuilders for his amazing leg development. His work-outs were the epitome of intensity. Here's how he'd achieve it:

Platz would constantly play mental tricks on himself during a set. While doing a set of squats, for instance, he would convince himself that his wife had been kidnaped and that someone was holding a gun to her head. Unless he completed the proscribed number of reps, she would be dead.

Can you imagine the intensity that you could generate if that was your reality? Well, it can be. Here are some other mental tricks that you can play on yourself in order to demand more from yourself during those final difficult reps:

(1) Tell yourself that a millionaire has just offered you $1 million to get that next rep.

(2) Picture an imaginary spotter who is standing over you, helping you to eke out that last rep.

(3) Imagine that an explosion has just occurred in the part of your body that you're working. Let the power of the blast explode you through that final rep (just don't sacrifice form on this one).

(4) Insult yourself. Sometimes a little bit of strategic negative self talk can work wonders. There's a classic scene in Pumping Iron where Arnold Schwarzenegger is spotting Franco Columbu on a set of bench presses. Franco gets the weight stuck on his chest and, rather than helping him, Arnold calls him a 'lazy bastard.' Franco then grits his teeth and powers the weight back up. You don't need Arnold around. Call yourself a lazy bastard (or the female version thereof).

(5) Make it a life or death experience. Picture yourself hanging off a cliff by your fingertips. If you can't get that weight up, then your grip is going to fail and it will all be over.

(6) Get angry with the weights. Consider that they are challenging you, mocking you. They are calling your a loser. Don't let them win. Be better than them. Call on your self pride and defeat those nasty pieces of iron.

(7) View yourself as the hardest worker in the gym (keep it to yourself, you might appear cocky). Imagine that everyone knows that you are the hardest trainer there. You have a reputation to live up to. Don't let them down.

Chapter Three

TRAINING FOR REAL MUSCLE MASS

The key to building, and keeping, consistent muscle mass is variety. The best program in the world for you will give you results for only so long. That's because our bodies are extremely adaptive. When they become acclimatized to a workout program, your results will diminish – and finally stop all together. That is why you will presented with two workout phases in this book:

Phase One: Foundational Mass Training

Phase Two: Peripheral Heart Action Training

YOUR 12 MONTH TRAINING PLAN

You will be alternating between these two workout systems over the course of the next 12 months. Begin with your Phase

One Program. Stick with it for 8 weeks, focusing on getting stronger while maintaining perfect form. At the end of 8 weeks, take a complete week off from training. Then go into your Phase Two Program. Work this program for a further 8 weeks. Then take another complete week off. Now go back to your Phase One Program for a further 8 weeks.

This Phase One / Phase Two rotation with a week's gap between each phase will allow you to complete 3 phases of each workout over the next 12 months.

PHASE ONE: FOUNDATIONAL MASS TRAINING

The bodybuilding magazines and websites have made building muscle extremely complicated (and extremely lucrative) to the extent that every guy thinks he needs to do at least 6 exercise for his biceps and triceps alone. Split routines are the default workout style. Anything less is for the pencil neck geek and the clueless klutz.

Let everyone else in the gym carry on their merry multi exercise, isolation focused way. You are going to train smarter. For a hard gainer to build muscle what's needed is increasing the weights, dropping the reps, taking longer rest periods between sets and to focus on the basic compound exercises. That's why

your entire routine is going to consist of the big 6 mass builders
. . .

Squats

Dead-lifts

Pull Ups

Bench Press

Military Press

That's it! No barbell curls, no pec dec flyes, no lying leg curls.
Put all of your energy and focus into the compound exercises that
are already working every muscle in your body.

What's more, you'll only be in the gym twice a week. Go
with Monday and Thursday, to provide maximum rest between
workouts. Do not be tempted to do more exercise than this -
it will be counter productive. Just make sure that every single
second of every workout is full on.

From now on, your training mindset needs to be: Get in, work
your body like hell, then get out.

Unless you get your choice of exercise right, you're going to
be wasting a lot of time in the gym for very little reward. Heavy
compound movements are the key to building muscle mass. These
are the multi-joint movements that work a variety of muscle

groups simultaneously. They also simulate real life movements, like squatting down or lifting something off the floor. Prime examples of compound movements are chin ups, squats and the bench press. These exercises are not only the best way to build bulk and they will get you stronger quicker than anything else. And, because they work muscle groups simultaneously, they are far more time efficient than isolation movements.

OPTIMIZED EXERCISE TECHNIQUE

The following exercises will form the basis of your training:

- Squats

- Dead-lifts

- Pull Ups

- Bench Press

- Military Press

Let's now take a close look at each of these core exercises:

SQUATS

Squats are known as a compound exercise, meaning that they target more than one muscle group. This simple movement does, in fact, directly stimulate every muscle group in the lower body. The prime movers, however, are the inner thighs, the butt and the hips. Indirectly, the squat even provides a workout to the muscles of the upper body. It also generates a great cardiovascular benefit. By taking deep breaths between each repetition and forcing the air out of the body on the ascent, the heart and lungs will be working overtime to support the work of the muscles of the body. This ensures that a ton of calories are being burnt and that the cardiovascular system is getting a rev up at the same time.

Preparation: Place an Olympic bar on the squat rack. At a weight of 45 lbs you won't need to add any added weight but make sure that use a pad in the middle of the bar to protect your neck.

Execution: Position yourself under the bar and lift it off the rack. Step back and stand with your feet spread slightly wider than shoulder width and pointing slightly outward. Keep your back straight, your chest thrust out and your head up. Now tense your abdominal wall, bend you knees and lower your body until your thighs are parallel with the floor. To avoid excess strain on the knees, don't go down any further. While squatting, keep your head up and your back slightly arched.

In the bottom squat position, your lower legs should be almost vertical to the floor. Push through your heels as you return to the starting position.

Breathing: Because squats include an aerobic component, it's vital that you use proper breathing technique. If you don't you may start to feel light headed after a few repetitions. As you lower yourself, breath in deeply. Then on the way back up, forcefully expel the air in one breath. During the final few repetitions, take two or three quick breaths between reps.

WHAT NOT TO DO WHEN YOU SQUAT

- Squatting over a bench. Every time you touch the bench with your glutes, your spine will compress slightly. Over time this may cause vertebral damage.

- Placing a block under your heels / turning your toes too widely outwards. Both of these will place unnatural stresses on your knees and, over time, can lead to injury.

- Leaning too far forward. Not only does this increase your likelihood of suffering spinal injuries, it also takes the stress off the quadriceps and onto the trunk extensor muscles.

- Allowing the knees to ride over the toes while allowing your heels to lift off the floor. Keeping your lower legs almost vertical may feel unnatural at first but it can make the difference between injured and healthy knees. Keeping your shin bones vertical drastically reduces your risk of injury.

DEAD-LIFTS

Often referred to as the king of exercises, the barbell deadlift is an extremely effective mass builder. It specifically targets the legs and back, but will place secondary adaptive stress upon nearly every muscle group in your body. Here's how to perform them correctly:

Squat down so your feet are under the bar, and the bar rests against your shins. Grip the bar using an alternate hook grip to prevent it from rotating. Your hands should be a little wider than shoulder width apart. Make sure to keep your back flat and tight throughout the movement.

Begin lifting the bar with a long, strong leg push, extending your knees and hips. Your knees should be bent as you lift the bar past them. Pull your shoulder blades together as you do this. Push your hips in toward the bar and keep the bar close to your body throughout the lift.

Continue the lift as if pushing the floor away from you with your feet, unless you stand up straight with your knees locked. Brace your shoulders back as you lift. Also make sure that you grip the bar tightly, so that it doesn't rotate in your hand.

With your knees unlocked, and maintaining a tight, flat back and keep your head up, start to lower the bar under control. Your knees should be bent as you lower the bar past them. Move your hips back and down as you descend.

Slowly move your hips and shoulder together when lowering the bar back down to the start position. Do not drop the bar. Make sure that you are bending at the knees and pulling your shoulders back.

Correct lifting technique is essential with this movement. Never lift with your spine flexed forward. Not only will the exercise be ineffective if you do, but you also risk spinal injury. Always raise and lower your shoulders and hips together. Keep the bar close to your body and do not drop it at the end of the movement. Always lower the bar under control.

DUMBBELL VARIATION

Using dumbbells for the deadlift recruits more muscles to control and stabilize movement. It is a good way of developing strength and technique for heavier barbell lifts. Start with light weights to determine your range of motion. As with the barbell lift, keep your back flat and the weights close to your body. Do not pause at the bottom of the movement or allow the weights to 'bounce' as you lower them.

WIDE GRIP PULL UPS

Wide Grip Pull Ups to the front are a great movement to widen the upper back and create a full sweep in the lats. Chinning yourself so that you touch the chest to the bar rather than the back of the neck gives you a slightly longer range of motion and is less strict, allowing you to cheat slightly so that you can continue your reps even after you are tired.

Method:

Take hold of the chinning bar with an overhand grip, hands as wide apart as practicable.

Hang from the bar, then pull yourself up, trying to touch the top of your chest to the bar. At the top of the movement, hold for a brief moment, then lower yourself back to the starting position.

TIPS FOR MAXIMUM RESULTS

- ✓ Pay attention to the details so that you can extract the most from the movement. Let your legs hang down straight, and don't jerk your way up. Just pull yourself up in a smooth motion, then let your body down under control. Jerking movements shift the effort, taking tension off the lats.

- ✓ For maximum stretch and contraction, lower yourself to the very bottom of each rep and pull up until the bar touches the chest (or your chin in the later reps of the set).

- ✓ A grip just outside the shoulders is very effective. However, you should vary it to stimulate the muscle somewhat differently. The wide grip invites the tendency to do half reps, but better development comes with full range ones.

- ✓ As you move your grip on the pull up bar closer to your midline, the greater the lower lat development along with the intercostals. Try a series of sets, starting with and finishing narrow, inching your grip closer with the set.

✓ Shoot for a specific number of reps, say 50, rather than counting sets. On the first set you may do 10 reps. Perhaps you struggle with eight on the second set. You've now got 18 reps. If you make five on the third set, you're up to 23 reps. Continue to add them until you have reached 50, even though it may take you 20 sets to do it. That will allow you to build both size and power.

✓ After you've mastered 10-12 reps in any type of pull up, you can start to put weight around your waist. That's when the muscle really begins to grow. Add about ten pounds at a time, which should make the reps harder. As you become stronger, ad more weight. It's only when you are able to start adding weight that your last will really grow!

BENCH PRESS

The bench press is a key compound mass builder for the entire body. It places you in a position of power, enabling you to lift very heavy weight and, therefore, exert maximum stress on the working muscles. While its major target is the chest, it also works the triceps, the shoulders and the back. In other words, it gives a damn good workout to your entire upper body.

Before we delve into the specifics of bench press performance, let's make it clear what our goal is. We're interested in building muscle, right? The bench is a tool towards that end. That is why we refer to ourselves as bodybuilders rather than power-lifters. For power-lifters the weight itself is the goal and that means that the exercise, although bearing the same name, is performed in a quite different way to a person who is using it as a tool to work their body. The being said, how do we use the bench press to build muscle?

Here's the basic technique:

Lie on a bench with your head, torso and hips resting against it and your feet planted on the floor. Take a hold of the bar with a full overhand grip and with your arms slightly wider than shoulder width. Lift the bar off the rack so that it is being supported above your collar bone.

Pulling your shoulder blades together, slowly lower the bar to just above your nipples. Press back up in a slightly arcing movement until the bar returns to it's starting position. Stop just short of lock-out and remember to keep your shoulder blades pulled back.

The following tips will allow you to optimize your technique:

> ➢ Either place a four inch block under your feet or position your feet on the bench. This will lessen the likelihood of back arch during the movement as well as preventing your quads from taking some of the load that should be going to your chest.

> ➢ After taking a grip on the bar which is wide enough so that your forearms are not quite parallel, lift it off the rack and, with it positioned above your mid chest, pinch your shoulder blades together.

> ➢ Lower the bar to the sternum (that is, just below the nipples). Your elbows should end up at 70 degree angles to your sides and your forearms should be vertical.

> ➢ Touch your chest (never bounce), forcefully stretch your pecs and immediately drive upwards, squeezing your lats and arcing the bar up to its start position at mid chest. Lock out briefly between reps. Keep your shoulders down throughout the pressing movement.

> ➢ Breathing: inhale while the bar is overhead, hold your breath during the descent and breathe out as you press back up.

FIVE THINGS TO NEVER DO ON THE BENCH

Bring the bar down to your upper chest. It will place way too much harmful stress on your shoulders and could, if done repeatedly, land you in line for surgery – which is definitely not recommended.

1. Perform hip thrusts. The hips MUST stay down on the bench. If they don't, not only are you wasting the exercise, you are also courting major lower spinal disc problems.

2. Use a thumbless grip. It keeps the wrist hyper-extended, making it more injury prone. The thumbless grip also makes it easier to lose control of the bar as well as giving you less grip strength. All of which gives it the big thumbs down.

3. Let momentum do the work. It should go without saying that every exercise in the gym needs to be done with a controlled movement. Momentum negates your effort, robbing you of results and fooling yourself into thinking that you're strong. In addition, it's dangerous – especially when you're handling heavy poundages. Bottom line – NEVER bounce the bar off your chest when benching.

4. Twist your neck around – no matter how hot that babe who just came into your peripheral vision looks. If you

do you're just asking for trouble – a guaranteed recipe for remaining dateless and desperate.

MILITARY PRESS

The military press is the granddaddy of all shoulder exercises. It directly hits the front and side deltoids, to give you both shoulder width and thickness. When you do the movement from a seated position the movement will be stricter than when standing.

Basic Military Press technique:

From a sitting position, grasp a barbell with an overhand grip and hold it at shoulder level, pams underneath for support, hands outside your shoulders, elbows tucked in and under.

From a position about even with your collarbone, lift the bar straight up overhead until your arms are locked out, being careful to keep the weight balanced and under control. Lower the weight back to the start position.

OPTIMIZED MILITARY PRESS TECHNIQUE:

From the bottom position, move your elbows forward so that they are actually in front of your torso, rather than flared back. This will take the focus of stress from your upper back and place it on your delts. This will also relieve a lot of the tension from your spine. This may require you to drop back the weight slightly. The enhanced delt focus, however, will more than compensate.

EXTRA TIPS:

USE A WIDE GRIP (TOO NARROW A GRIP SHIFTS THE FOCUS TO THE TRICEPS)

Do not lock out at the top of the movement

Keep your back arched throughout

Do not bounce the weight off your chest

THE WORKOUT

Now that you've got to grips with the proper performance of each of the exercises in your back to foundational mass training workout, let's take a look at how to put them together to ensure maximum results. Remember that you'll be working the whole body in each session and training twice per week. The ideal training days will allow for a minimum of two full rest days between them.

Rep & Set Scheme

FOR EVERY EXERCISE, EXCEPT FOR PULL UPS, USE THE FOLLOWING REP SCHEME:

Warm Up – 15 reps

Working sets – 12 reps

10 reps

8 reps

6 reps

For Pull Ups, set yourself a target of 30 reps in the first two weeks. Do this is as few sets as possible, as described in the Pull Ups exercise description. After two weeks, up the target to 40 reps. After two more weeks, lift it once more to 50 reps.

Both research and experience have shown that bodybuilders get the most muscle building benefit from training with a weight that is between 70 and 75 percent of their one rep maximum. Your one rep max is the amount of weight that you can lift while doing one full-out rep with perfect form. When you pyramid your reps, as you will be doing, you slightly increase the weight as you decrease the reps.

The weight that you choose should mean that you are training to failure one ach set. This means that you will be continuing the set until you can't do any more reps with that weight without stopping to rest.

You'll be doing 4 working sets on each exercise (apart from pull ups, which will take as many sets as required to hit your target). You need to do at least 4 sets in order to have the volume of training necessary to fully stimulate all of the available muscle. If you do more sets per exercise, your total training volume will be so great that you risk over training.

WORKOUT A: FOUNDATIONAL MASS TRAINING

EXERCISE	REPS
Squats	15 – 12 / 10 / 8 / 6
Deadlift	15 – 12 / 10 / 8 / 6
Pull Ups	Total 30 reps
Bench Press	15 – 12 / 10 / 8 / 6
Military Press	15 – 12 / 10 / 8 / 6

HOW LONG?

You should continue on this training program for 8 weeks. That will be long enough for you to should some real improvement in your strength and muscle gains, but not too long to bring on diminishing returns due to over familiarization.

At the end of eight weeks, take a complete week off from training before moving into your Phase Two program.

PHASE TWO: PERIPHERAL HEART ACTION TRAINING

Peripheral Heart Action Training has been around since the 1940's, when it was developed by Dr Arthur Steinhaus. It was popularised in the '60's by Mr Universe title holder Bob Gajda. PHA is designed to keep the blood circulating around the entire body during the workout. Even though it may sound like circuit training, it is actually a very intense and a very effective way to pack muscle mass onto your body. Unlike circuit training, PHA requires that you use heavy weight and that you stick with good form.

This is a great workout option for hard gainers. PHA training will give your muscles an amazing pump. By shunting the blood around the body, you will also be receiving some important neuromuscular effects. The varied rep and target muscle scheme creates greater neurological pathways to the working muscle. This increases blood flow to the muscle.

PHA training is built around compound movements – like the ones you've been using during your Phase One training. A major goal of your workout will be to shunt the blood around your body.

Because you will be doing consecutive sets for different body parts, you will be allowing the target muscle more rest than with conventional training. This will allow you to use neat maximal strength output on each and every set.

With PHA training you need to be focusing on making your workout more intense with each and every session. Here's how to do that:

➢ push out more reps with the same weight

➢ do more sequences within the same time space

➢ put more weight on the bar

Performing PHA training with basic, compound multi-joint exercises like squats, deadlifts, and overhead presses will be extremely hard work. In fact, the reason that PHA training is not used more frequently is simply that it is too damned hard for most people to be able to handle for any length of time. But you're not most people – right?

HOW DOES PHA WORK?

Peripheral Heart Action training involves doing tri-sets of exercises. This means that you do one set of an exercise, then move directly to another exercise for a different body part, followed by a final exercise for a third body part. After a rest period, you go on to your next tri-set. The workout usually consists of two or three of these tri sets to work the entire body.

In this program you will be completing three sets of two tri sets per workout. This is intense training, as you move straight from one exercise to the next without any rest. At the end of your tri set, you rest for two to three minutes before you move to your next set.

You will be training every other day on this program. Remember that the exercises that are grouped together in your tri set is not for the same body part. You will be either performing Workout 1 or Workout 2, alternating them each workout.

THE PHA REP SCHEME

A unique aspect of the PHA System that you are about to embark upon is the tailored rep scheme. Each exercise in a tri set has its own rep count. Here's how it works:

Exercise One: The first exercise that you will do in each tri set will be done for 5 reps. That means that you will be using a very heavy weight on that movement. You should not go to failure, however.

Exercise Two: The second exercise will be done for a rep count of between 8 and 12. Start with a weight that will allow 8 good reps. As you get stronger, increase the reps until you can do 12. At that point increase the weight to the extent that you are again only able to pump out 8 reps.

Exercise Three: The third exercise in your tri set will involve doing between 15 and 20 reps. This will gorge the muscle with blood, providing an amazing pump.

WORKOUT B: PERIPHERAL HEART ACTION (PHA)

WORKOUT 1

TRI-SET A	
SQUATS	3 X 5-8
DUMBBELL INCLINE PRESS	3 X 8-12
UPRIGHT ROWING	3 X 15-20
TRI-SET B	
PULL UPS	3 X 5-8
DUMBBELL CURLS	3 X 8-12
FLYES	3 X 15-20

NOTE: Always perform a light warm-up set on the first movement of each tri-set.

WORKOUT 2

TRI-SET A	
DEADLIFT	3 X 5-8
CALF RAISES	3 X 8-12
SIDE LATERAL RAISES	3 X 15-20
TRI-SET B	
DUMBBELL SHOULDER PRESS	3 X 5-8
LUNGES	3 X 8-12
TRICEP PUSHDOWNS	3 X 15-20

THE EXERCISES

Some of the exercises that you will be using in your PHA training phase are familiar to you from your Phase One program. In this section we outline the proper technique for those that are not.

DUMBBELL INCLINE PRESS

If the incline bench you are using is adjustable, set it to a very steep angle (no more than 30 degrees from vertical). The steep angle focuses the exercise on the uppermost section of the pecs. Bring the dumbbells up to your chest level. In the starting position the weights should be resting against your shoulders.

Press the dumbbells up, using the pecs to pull the arm up and cross the chest. Following this path makes the exercise more stable and puts minimum emphasis on the main synergist, the triceps. Keep your back flat against the bench as you lift.

At the top of the movement, hunch your shoulders forward and up to unsure that you get complete pec stimulation. Lower the dumbbells back to the starting point. At the bottom of the movement, feel for a stretch in the delts and pecs.

UPRIGHT ROW

If you have access to a pulley machine, use it for this exercise. Otherwise a barbell will do.

Hold the barbell or pulley bar in the middle, palms down, hands touching one another. Stand directly above the pulley, if possible. Pull straight up until your arms are at shoulder level. Keep the bar close to the body. If you pull up with the bar away from the body, the exercise focuses on the anterior delt only. Hold for a second and then lower and repeat.

DUMBBELL CURLS

Begin with a dumbbell in each hand, palms facing back. You can increase your stability and decrease general strain during the exercise by performing the movement leaning against a bench with your knees slightly bent.

Think of the exercise as a combination of two movements that must be smoothly integrated. First, supination of the forearm. This is simply rotating the forearm so your palm, which begins facing backward, ends up facing forward.

Second, a curl. Proper curling form is not obvious, nor is it what the body naturally does, if given a chance. The natural tendency with any exercise is to do as little work as possible. When doing curls, for example, your body adjusts to the position of greatest mechanical advantage, taking as much strain off your biceps as possible – not at all what you want to develop your biceps.

To maximize the work done by your biceps during any curl you must make sure that your elbows remain in close to the body. Moving the elbow away from the body takes most of the strain off the biceps and puts possibly damaging stress on the elbows. You should also keep your elbow slightly in front of you during the curl. The natural tendency is to let the elbow move next to the body – or worse, behind the body – as you raise the weight. This also takes the strain off the body.

When performing a supinated curl, both the supination of the forearm and the curling motion should occur simultaneously. The supination should not happen all at once. Try to rotate the forearm smoothly throughout the entire curling motion. Remember to bring your elbow in front of you to ensure maximum action of the long head of the bicep, which flees the shoulder as well as the elbow.

Lean into the curl at the top to keep tension on the biceps.

On the way down it is important to exactly reverse the movement performed on the way up.

FLYES

Lie face up on a flat bench. Rest your feet on the end of the bench to prevent your back from arching during the exercise. Grasp a dumbbell in each hand and extend your hands straight up, palms facing each other. Your elbows should not be bent.

Lower the weights to each side to just below the level of the bench. The weights – and your arms – should remain perpendicular to your body through your shoulders. Feel for the stretch across the midline of the pecs. Your arms should end up at right angles to your body. To minimize potentially harmful strain on your biceps and elbows, your elbows should be slightly bent at the bottom of the motion, with your arms above bench level.

Moving in the largest arc possible, bring the weights back up to the starting position. Keep your arms within the ideal plane. Do not increase the bend in the elbows. If you do, the emphasis will shift from the pecs to the triceps. At the peak of the movement, your shoulders should come up off the bench slightly as you bring the weights together.

Concentrate on feeling the exercise across your chest and not in your shoulders.

CALF RAISES

Stand with your toes on the block of a standing calf raise machine, your heels extending out into space. Hook your shoulders under the pads and straighten your legs, lifting the weight clear of the support. Lower your heels as far as possible toward the floor, keeping your knees slightly bent throughout the movement in order to work the lower area of the calves as well as the upper area, and feeling the calf muscles stretch to the maximum. From the bottom of the movement, come up on your toes as far as possible. The weight should be heavy enough to exercise the calves, but not so heavy that you cannot come all the way up for most of your repetitions.

SIDE LATERAL RAISES

Hold two dumbbells, one in each hand, at your sides, palms facing your sides. Lift the weights out to the side, pretending that, instead of dumbbells, you have pitchers of water in each hand and that you are going to water some plants up at shoulder level.

Allow your elbows to bend and your forearms to drive slightly forward out of the ideal plane. As you reach the top of the movement, rotate your shoulders forward so the front plates of the dumbbells are slightly lower than the rear plates – just as if you were pouring water. This will raise your elbows slightly. The rotation should come from your shoulders, not your wrists or arms.

The pouring motion positions the lateral deltoid to take the brunt of the strain. If you don't pour, the Anterior Deltoid helps out too much, decreasing the efficiency of the exercise.

DUMBBELL SHOULDER PRESS

Sitting on a bench, hold one dumbbell in each hand at shoulder height, elbows out to the side, palms facing forward. Lift the dumbbells straight up until they touch at the top, then lower them again as far as possible. You will find that you are able to both raise and lower the dumbbells farther than you can a barbell, although the need to control two weights independently means that you are lifting slightly less poundage.

Lunges

Stand with your feet hip-width apart, and hold two dumbbells at your sides. Take a bold stride forward, far enough so that your front thigh ends up parallel to the floor with your knees over (but not past) your toes. Quickly push back up to the starting position. Alternate legs, counting both legs as one rep.

Triceps Pushdowns

Hook a short bar to an overhead cable and pulley, stand close to the bar and grasp it with an overhand grip, hands about 10 inches apart. Keep your elbows locked in close to your body and stationary. Keep your whole body steady – don't lean forward to press down with your body weight.

Press the bar down as far as possible, locking out your arms and feeling the triceps fully contracting. Release and let the bar come up as far as possible without moving the elbows. For variety, you can vary your grip, the type of bar you use, how close you stand to the bar, or the width between your hands.

Chapter Four

THE TRAINING PARTNER FACTOR

The sweat trickles down his forehead. The calloused hands tighten on the bar. He bites his lip and focuses on the 500 pounds of cold steel hovering over his body. The grip tightens and he eases the bar off of its support rack. Slowly, but steadily, the weight descends to his sternum . . .

As the bar kisses his sweat soaked t-shirt, his triceps come into action and the weight begins to rise. Two inches from his body, however, the bar stops. He has reached the sticking point - the moment on the lift that is the most difficult. Now, with more than a quarter-ton threatening to splinter his ribcage into a thousand pieces, he surges every fiber of his being into the fray. A Neanderthal grunt escapes his throat as his massive chest swells the t-shirt to breaking point. But the weight refuses to budge. Sensing failure he glances skyward. Within that moment the reassuring fingers of his training partner gently glide the bar upward past the sticking point and it's easy now. He can glide the weight back to it's staring position.

He's ready for one more rep . . .

Take the partner out of that equation and what have you got? At best a set that finishes too early - at worst a severely injured iron pumper. All of which would seem to suggest that a bodybuilder without a training partner is a bit like a smoke detector without batteries - it looks the part but it's just not up to the job. But hang on a minute - isn't bodybuilding meant to be the ultimate isolationist sport? In fact, didn't the great one himself (that's Governor great one to you) once admit that he gravitated to it because he didn't want to share the glory with others? Well, yes but he was also a part of one of the hottest training partnerships in the history of muscledom. Hey - when you've won 7 Mr Olympia's, you're allowed a few contradictory statements. So much for him - what about you? Should you put out for a partner or continue hitting the plates as a lone wolf?

ARE TWO REALLY BETTER THAN ONE?

Two are better than one because they have a good reward for their hard work. For if one of them should fall, the other can raise his partner up. But how will it be with just the one who falls when there is not another to raise him up?

Sounds like good bodybuilding advice, right? Well, in fact, those words were written over 3,000 years ago in the Bible (no, we're not referring to Bill Pearl's Keys to the Inner Universe - were talking about the REAL Bible, Ecclesiastes 4:9,10 to be exact). So, how about it? Does the revealed wisdom of the Creator translate to the gym floor? Why not check out the pros and cons and decide for yourself?

PARTNER POSITIVES

SAFETY:

The number one advantage of a training partner is that they are there to protect you if you get into trouble under the heavy iron. Serious bodybuilding equals heavy lifting and pushing a set to failure and beyond. Without a partner you simply cannot do that as efficiently. Sure, you can always ask the guy working out next to you for a spot when you think you're going to need one, but unless a spotter is tuned into you and your specific needs, nine times out of ten their help will actually ruin the set for you, either by giving too much assistance or by causing the bar to ascend unevenly. A partner who knows how to spot you will do the job properly.

MOTIVATION:

It doesn't matter how dedicated we are to packing mass onto our frames, all of us have times when we're dragging the chain, when just getting to the gym is a monumental effort, when our warm-up set feels like a ton, when we're on auto-pilot and can't wait to get out of the place. A good partner can be the perfect antidote to these stale, unproductive patches. For a start, just knowing that someone is going to be waiting for you gives most people (those with a least a spark of conscience, anyway) a kick in the butt out the door. And unless you've teamed up with the clinically depressed, the odds are that they'll show up with some of the energy that you're lacking. That energy could be the very thing you need to transform a by the numbers work-out (in other words, a total waste of your time) into a muscle quivering growth explosion.

COMPETITION:

We humans thrive on competition - it brings out the best and the worst in us. Having a training partner can allow you to put that piece of psychology to use in your muscle building endeavors. You can push each other to your limits, try to outdo each other and even go crazy once in a while. Schwarzenegger and Columbu, for instance, used to have curl fests where they'd load up a bar and then one of them would do as many strict curls as he could. After the last rep he'd literally throw the bar at his partner who'd try to do one more rep that what he'd done. This would go on until one of them either punked out or passed out. The shock factor to their biceps allowed them to blast through plateaus and keep stretching that tape measure. Stuff like that every now and again will make your workouts more exciting and more productive.

ON THE OTHER HAND . . .

WASTED TIME:

It's an all too familiar scenario . . . you're on the go. You've got work to finish off at home tonight, a wife who needs affection and a couple of kids who are hanging out for their bed time story. So what the hell are you doing standing around waiting for that bozo workout partner to make an appearance? Throw in the fact that workouts are going to take longer and, unless you're careful, you could easily lose the advantage of zero rest time between sets on certain techniques like pre-exhaustion and super setting, and the time factor becomes a real issue.

BAD TECHNIQUE:

Some people just don't how to spot - no matter how many times you try to show them. Having a bad spotter is infinitely worse than not having one at all. If they take too much of the weight, your set is ruined. And if they focus on the babe on the leg adductor machine instead of the weight in your hand, your set, not to mention your potential well being, is on the skids once again.

DIFFERENT MINDSETS:

Finding partner who wants to build muscle may not be that difficult. But how about finding one who's willing to get out of bed at 5:30 every morning, who's open minded enough to try training routines that fly in the face of what they think they know and who've got the guts and determination to consistently push through the pain barrier. It ain't that easy.

INTERNAL MOTIVATORS:

Tom Platz retired from competitive bodybuilding well over a decade ago. Yet, he's still revered as one of the hardest trainers of all time. Funny thing is, his motivation didn't come from a training partner. From within himself, Platz was able to summon up seemingly super human qualities of concentration, focus and intensity. Platz would play mind games on himself wherein his temporary reality would be that his wife had been kidnapped and would be killed if he didn't get a certain number of reps on a certain exercise that he was doing. The results were legendary workouts. Needless to say, Platz was the ultimate lone wolf. A partner would have ruined his ability to concentrate. There are many such individuals who are able to fully self-motivate and to whom a partner would be nothing short of a pain in the gluteus maximus.

PROGRAM CONFLICTS:

So, your weak point is your upper pecs. Your partner, however - well you could balance a glass of water on his damned pecs and not spill a drop. His delts, however, are another story. Unlike yours, they've got no width. Clearly you've got different weak points. A good program should be built around hammering weak points first, but what's a guy to do when he and his partner have different areas of priority. Compromises will necessarily have to be made which could led to less than optimum workouts.

AND THE VERDICT IS . . .?

Now that we've got you nice and confused, what are you going to decide - partner or solo? First determine if you're a self motivator or a guy who thrives on external input. If you've got that Platz-like ability to summon up super-human energy, by all means go it alone. Talk to an instructor at the gym and explain to them that you prefer to train alone but that you'll be calling on them for a spot when you go real heavy. If they're any good at their job they'll be happy to oblige and they'll know how to spot you properly. If they're not, then what the hell are you doing there?

Everyone else should seriously consider a training partner. They key, however, is to be selective. Get the wrong guy and your muscle building goals are in jeopardy. Here's a checklist of qualities that you'll want to have ticks beside if you've found the right partner. Have a trial of a couple of weeks and see how he goes . . .

HOW DOES HE RATE?

TIMELINESS:

If the guys not there at least a couple of minutes before the scheduled start time of your workout, every workout for the first two weeks, can him. The first time he's late, start your workout on time and let him jump in when he arrives - he'll know you mean business.

CONSISTENCY:

Worse than being late is not showing up at all. A missed day during that trial period means the guy's a total loser. Move on.

MODESTY:

The last thing you want when you're trying to focus is some goof spewing on about how great they are. In fact, those idiots who don't know when to shut up and concentrate are even worse. So, if he suffers from verbal diarrhea, give him the shove.

ABILITY TO MOTIVATE:

He doesn't have to bark catch phrases at you like a drill sergeant, but he should be able to gently say the right words at the right time to help you achieve at the highest level. He should now, after those first two weeks, what buttons to push to get you to push out those critical last couple of reps.

COMPARABLE STRENGTH LEVELS:

You don't want to be flipping 20 pounders on and off between sets, so look for a guy who's about as strong as you are, maybe even just a little stronger. The exception to this is the extra motivation a guy can get from working out with a female. It's a proven fact that female partners give a male trainer the extra motivation to lift more - after all, who wants to fail in front of a girl?

Chapter Five

EATING TO GET HUGE

As the title of this chapter implies, your goal with eating over the next 12 months will be to gain muscular size. Despite the marketing that we see all around us about how you can get ripped while packing on mass, that is not what you are after right now. As a hard gainer, you cannot realistically get six pack abs while putting a dozen pounds of muscle mass onto your frame.

To gain muscle mass, you need to train hard and smart. You also need to give your body the time to recover, replenish and rebuild. The third ingredient is fuel, in the form of nutrition. If you are taking in more quality calories than you are burning, then the balance will be utilized to build muscle mass.

This doesn't mean that you are going to throw yourself into the old school bulking up mentality. Clearly all calories are not equal. Gaining weight is not your goal here – gaining lean muscle mass is what this is all about. That's why you will be eating clean nearly all of the time.

Neither will you indulge in an one the current crop of fad diets that are promulgating cyberspace right now. Intermittent fasting, the Keto diet or anything else that hits your inbox may work for some. But for you, as a hard gainer, right now it simply doesn't apply. You are going to stick with a basic balanced, macronutrient program based on calories per day.

YOUR MAINTENANCE CALORIE LEVEL

In order to determine how many calories you need to be consuming each day, you need to firstly work out how many calories you need to be taking in just to function. Everything you do , from breathing to scratching your nose, burns calories. If you don't take in enough calories to meet these needs, then you will find yourself in a catabolic state (not a good place to be).

A simple formula to allow you to work out your maintenance calorie level is to multiply your current bodyweight in kilograms by 24.

Alternatively, multiply your current bodyweight in pounds by 0.45, then by 24

Let's take a 180 pound guy. First we'll multiply his bodyweight by 0.45 to get his weight in kilograms . . .

180 x 0.45 = 81 kilograms

Now, we do the second calculation . . .

81 x 24 = 1944

So, we now know that our 180 pound guy requires about 1950 calories per day to maintain his current bodyweight and supply the energy for his activities over a 24 hour period.

Our goal, of course, is not to maintain our body weight. We want to add muscle mass. We don't want to add too many calories, as we are conscious of putting on lean mass only. A sensible amount to shoot for is 300 extra calories per day. 300 calories is manageable, without leaving your feel bloated. Yet, over the course of 12 months (and you need to be thinking of this as a year long program), you will have taken in an extra 109,500 calories. This will provide your body with a whole of quality fuel for building muscle.

So, let's go back to our 180 pound guy, and add our extra calorie count . . .

1944 + 300 = 2244

We now have our daily calorie count of around 2250 calories per day.

Now, clearly, you aren't going to take all of those calories into your body in one huge meal. But, neither should you do so over the course of three meals. To provide prime fuel for your body you need to give it a continual supply of nutrients. In fact you should be feeding it every two and a half hours. So, that is what you'll be doing. You'll learn more about why and how your should be eating every two-three hours in Chapter Six, but for now you need to establish how many calories you should be consuming at each meal.

To do this, we simply divide your total calorie figure by six.

So, for our 180 pound guy . . .

2244 / 6 = 374 calories

Our 180 pound hard gainer needs to be consuming 374 calories every meal, with meals spaced three hours apart.

MACRONUTRIENT BREAKDOWN

The three macro-nutrients in our foods are proteins, carbohydrates and fats. Well examine them in more detail in the next chapter. Our job right now is to establish the ideal ratio between these foods for each of your six meals.

Carbohydrates are the energy source that your body relies upon for everything that it does. Carbs are especially important for those, like you, who are engaged in hard, intense weight resistance training.

Protein, of course, is essential for building muscle. Everything in your body is composed of amino acids, the building blocks of protein. In order to recover from your workouts and rebuild your body, you need to ensure that a steady supply of quality protein is flowing through your blood stream.

Fats come in good and bad varieties. The good fats are known as essential fatty acids (EFA's). The two primary categories of EFA's are omega-3 and omega-6. You need them for a whole host of health, wellness and muscle building benefits. The best sources are fatty fish like salmon, sardines herring, mackerel and rainbow trout as well as flaxseeds, walnuts, fish oil, avocado and flaxseed oil.

The ideal macronutrient for the hard gainer bodybuilder is ...

50% CARBS / 30% PROTEIN / 20% FATS

That means that, at every meal, half of your plate should be filled with complex and fibrous carbs, three fifths of the other half should consist of a quality lean protein and the balance should be a healthy fat.

NUTRITION GUIDELINES SUMMARY

➤   Have your first meal when you first get up in the morning, then space them out every two and a half hours, i.e. . .

7am

9:30am

12pm

2:30pm

5:00pm

7:30pm

➤   Don't skip meals – work the plan. In the next chapter, you'll find some great ideas on how you can ensure that you get in very single meal, even when you're on the go!

➤   Cut out calorie laden beverages. Stick with water.

➤   Make wise use of liquid protein supplements. They are great way to help you get your protein and calories while you're on the run. Don't have more than two meals per day in the form of protein shakes, however.

➤   Count calories for the first couple of weeks. From there you should be able to gauge your meal sizes by sight.

➤   Allow your self one cheat meal every seven days. Make it a midday meal if possible. Enjoy yourself, but don't go too crazy!

➤   Make sure that your post workout meal allows you to get quality protein and carbs into your body within twenty minutes of finishing the workout.

Chapter Six

THE ANABOLIC ADVANTAGE: 9 WAYS TO GET IT

When it comes to muscle, your body knows two processes – anabolism and catabolism. They are the ying and yang of bodybuilding. The positive and the negative. The building up and the tearing down.

You goal is to be in a state of anabolism as often as possible. To build muscle that's where you need to be. Working out hard is not enough. Unless you've got all of the other factor in place, that sweat and strain will be all for nothing. So, what are these other vital factors that will determine whether your efforts in the gym will translate to mass on your frame?

By ensuring that the following 9 factors are taken care of consistently your body will be in the prime state to build muscle mass – the anabolic state. . .

FACTOR ONE: BE PROTEIN POSITIVE

Your muscles contain about 40% of the protein in your body. It is the raw material from which you are constructed. It is crucial in the rebuilding and recovery process. Yet, the consuming of protein, in itself, does not build muscle. It needs to be just one in a whole continuum of factors that work synergistically to bring about the end result of more mass on your frame.

Muscle growth can only occur if muscle protein synthesis exceeds muscle protein breakdown. This means that there must be a positive muscle protein balance. Strength training improves muscle protein balance, but, in the absence of food, the balance will remain negative, or catabolic.

The ingredient within protein which makes it so vital in the muscle building process is nitrogen. Unlike carbohydrates and fats, protein contains nitrogen, which is essential for the replacement of body cells. To be able to build muscle, and even to keep the muscle that we currently have, we must be in a state of positive nitrogen balance. That means that we need to be taking more nitrogen into our bodies than we are expending in the course of our daily activities.

If proteins are the building blocks of the body, then the building blocks of protein are amino acids. There are 20 amino acids that can be reformulated in a vast number of ways to create hundreds of different proteins. A dozen of these amino acids are able to be produced naturally by the human body. They are known as non essential amino acids because we don't have to rely on outside food sources to get them into our body.

The remaining 8 amino acids are known as essential because they can't be manufactured by the body and must come by way of the food we eat.

Here are the eight essential amino acids:

- Lysine

- Isoleucine

- Leucine

- Methionine

- Phenylaline

- Threonine

- Tryptophan

- Valine

Proteins sources that contain all eight of the essential amino acids are referred to as complete proteins. Many complete proteins come from animal sources. That's because an animal's molecular structure is similar to a human being. Here are some great animal sources of complete protein:

- Chicken Breast

- Salmon

- Turkey Breast

- Lean Beef – flank steak, bison, sirloin, lean ground beef

- Low Fat Pork

The very best complete protein source of them all is the egg.

As a hard gainer, you should aim for 1.5 grams of protein for every pound of bodyweight. So, if you are currently 175 pounds, you should be taking in . . .

$175 \times 1.5 = 262.5$ grams of protein per day.

This consumption should be spread over the course of six or seven meals during the day. Your body can only absorb about 50 grams of protein at one sitting. By eating six meals per day, spaced about three hour apart, you will be able to get your daily protein requirement without any waste.

Our 175 pound guy will be taking in . . .

$262.5 / 6$ grams of protein per meal

That equates to 43.75 grams per meal. To give you an idea of how much of a certain food to consume in order to get your protein requirement in, a large egg contains 6 grams of protein, while most lean meats like beef, chicken, turkey and fish contain 6 grams of protein. Milk contains 1 gram of protein per fluid ounce.

FACTOR TWO: SUPPLEMENT FOR SIZE

WHY SUPPLEMENT?

The right supplements - taken at the right times - can help propel you to your bodybuilding and strength training goals by doing three things. They can increase your anabolic drive, improve your workload capacity and decrease your recovery time. Individually these factors can make a big difference. Put together they will work synergistically to power you towards your goals. Let's consider them one at a time:

ANABOLIC DRIVE

The word 'anabolic' refers to the body's ability to produce more muscle tissue. Anabolic drive involves the natural production of testosterone, growth hormone (GH), insulin-like growth factor-1 (IGF-1), insulin, thyroid, cortisol and other hormones and growth factors involved in muscle growth. For athletes, it refers to the body's ability to increase it's anabolic (or muscle producing) response to exercise, nutrition, supplements and other factors.

In the case of supplements, those targeted towards increasing the production of testosterone, growth hormone and insulin, and decreasing cortisol, will result in both anabolic and anti-catabolic effects, thus maximizing the anabolic drive.

WORKLOAD CAPACITY

Endurance or workload capacity involves your ability to maintain high quality training throughout a workout. If your capacity is limited and you don't have the energy, endurance or concentration necessary to train hard from the beginning of your workout to the end, it won't matter how well you manage the other components - nutrition, supplementation and rest. Your diet may be excellent. You may even be training properly six days a week, but if you don't have the overall energy and muscle endurance for a productive workout, you aren't going to experience maximal progress or muscle growth.

RECOVERY

This involves your ability to recover properly between sets as well as workouts. The goal is to ensure that the body recovers fully from the stimulus of exercise and to reduce the amount of time necessary for it to take place. Recovery is critical to muscle growth. Your body must recuperate from the catabolic process before productive protein synthesis can occur. The sooner you recover from a workout, the sooner your body can begin to respond to it and adapt by adding muscle.

When you don't recover from workouts, you can go into a state of chronic over training. You'll actually begin to lose muscle instead of gaining it. In the gym, you'll find yourself lacking the energy to do further sets at maximum ability. Even if you do manage to get through a workout without losing effort, your body still won't respond with the kind of adaptation you want - more muscle.

Certain supplements can have a strong effect on lowering recovery time and increasing muscle growth. Supplements targeting recovery can also help you handle additional stress in your training. If you want to extend workouts from four to six days a week, supplements can help you accelerate recovery to make those workouts productive. Similarly, if you're training for another sport, in addition to your bodybuilding and strength training endeavors, supplements might just spell the difference between being able to train for both effectively and having the dual training sabotage your progress in both areas.

ANTI-CATABOLISM

You can decrease the breakdown of muscle tissue both during and after exercise and thus provide potent anti-catabolic effects in several ways. A lot of substances and methods decrease muscle breakdown and have anti-catabolic effects; for example taking in adequate carbohydrates is known to have a protein sparing effect.

Certain supplements can also create an anti-catabolic effect. Cortisol is a necessary hormone and in plays a significant role in decreasing muscle stiffness and inflammation. Without normal and somewhat elevated cortisol levels, we couldn't even exercise properly - so it wouldn't matter what training, diet, drug or nutritional supplement regimen you followed. Yet, chronically elevated levels of cortisol have a catabolic effect on muscle and decreases the effect of anabolic hormones. Decreasing the amount of cortisol after exercise can provide you with an added anabolic boost by decreasing muscle tissue breakdown and increasing amino-acid influx and utilization by muscle cells. In addition, decreasing catabolism by using appropriate methods and supplements can dramatically increase protein synthesis and muscle mass.

Substances that decrease catabolism can have anabolic effects on muscle. But like growth hormone stimulation, many nutritional supplements can also have anti-catabolic effects. Increasing dietary calories and protein and using branch chain amino acids, glutamine, alanine and other amino acids, Vitamin C, beta-carotene and other anti-oxidant vitamins have been shown to lessen muscle breakdown.

Supplements can also be used to increase insulin, Growth Hormone, IGF-1 and testosterone levels, and decrease cortisol levels and decrease cortisol levels and other anti-catabolic factors at specific times to maximize increases in lean body mass.

CONVENIENCE

Let's face it – we're all busy. It's not easy to get 40 or so grams of whole food protein into our body every three waking hours. Quality protein supplements, while never as ideal as whole foods, can be a life saver in this regard. Low-carb protein supplements are available in powder forms, as ready to drink bottles or cans, and as protein bars. These options make it a whole lot of easier to fill your protein requirements. However, try not to use supplements for more than two of your six daily meals. The human body was designed to eat protein, not to drink it!

In Chapter Seven we will reveal the essential supplements that you need to pack on quality mass fast.

FACTOR THREE

TAKE ADVANTAGE OF THE ANABOLIC WINDOW

After your workout your body is screaming out for protein. Your intense training has created tiny tears in the muscle cell that need fixing and rebuilding. Muscle glycogen has been depleted as a result of your workout. In addition, your workout has drained your body of energy. Your muscles are craving nutrients. This creates a window of opportunity for you to boost the body's anabolic state. But beware – this window only lasts for twenty minutes.

Your body will begin the rebuilding through muscle protein synthesis and glycogen resynthesis immediately after the workout. This provides an ideal opportunity to provide protein and carbs to the muscle. So, don't wait an hour to refuel your body after your training is done. Get some quality protein and carbs into your system straight away – even before you hit the shower.

To ensure that the protein gets to the muscle as quickly as possible you should rely on liquid protein sources after your workout. But remember you also need carbs to replenish your energy stores. Use a protein / carb shake that you can mix in your shaker bottle and gulp down as you head toward the change room. Make sure that the protein is whey based, as this is the fastest acting and most bio-available protein that there is.

FACTOR FOUR

CURTAIL CARDIO

Exercise, while good for us, induces a catabolic response in the body. Simply put, it places stress upon the body which results in the breakdown of body tissue. If our exercise sessions go on for too long, or involve extra training on top of our weights workouts, we will find it very hard to stay in an anabolic state.

Your weight training workouts need to be hard, intense and short. You need to get in, work the muscles like hell, and then get out. Your whole body workouts should be over and done with inside of an hour. If you train for longer than that, you will be entering a state of catabolism.

When you are ready to focus on getting ripped you can venture into the cardio area of the gym. Until then, however, you have no place there. Your goal as a hard gainer right now is to pack solid mass onto your frame. Cardio exercise that burns up valuable calories and depletes your energy reserves will put you in a state of catabolism. That is not what you want.

You should also consider the amount of sport that you're playing. An hour of basketball every other day will not be conducive to either building muscle or staying in an anabolic state. If you are going to play sport, make sure that you replace the extra calories that you will be consuming. Remember that you will not build muscle if you are in a negative calorie balance.

FACTOR FIVE

GET YOUR COMPLEX CARBS

The poor old carbohydrate has gotten a bad rap. Over recent years, low carb diets have been touted as the solution to rapid weight loss. Believing that curbing the carbs will force the body to draw on their fat stores for energy, millions of people have extremely restricted their total carb intake while actually eating more fatty foods. For most of them, the fat stays where it is while their body starts eating into their muscle stores for that essential energy. It's about time that the carbohydrate started getting the respect it deserves. Maybe then people will begin to be able to eat their carbs in a manner that promotes leanness and health – as well as muscle gain.

CARBS PROMOTE ANABOLISM

Carbohydrates are complex sugar molecules that promote the release of insulin. Insulin is a potent anabolic hormone that transports amino acids into the muscle cell, to be utilized for repair and regrowth of the muscle. So, even if you are getting all the protein you need, without quality complex carbs, that protein will be a huge stack of coal sitting at the train depot – it won't have a transport system to get it into the muscle.

Carbohydrates are the body's preferred fuel source. The body can also use protein and fat for fuel but these macronutrients are far less efficient at providing the body with the energy it needs. All the carbs that you eat end up in your blood as glucose or blood sugar. Yet not all carbs are equal.

SIMPLE VS COMPLEX CARBS

The two broad categories of carbs are simple and complex. Simple carbs are made up of either a single sugar molecule or two sugar molecules linked together. They provide very little in the way of vitamin or mineral content. They are easily digested by the body and provide an immediate energy boost. This leads to an increase of the release of insulin in the pancreas. The insulin does the job of clearing the glucose from the bloodstream with the result that weak, low in energy and hungry. This leads to a repeat cycle of binging on more simple carbs and the whole process starts over. Simple carbs are not your friend.

Complex carbs are made up of many molecules and are known as polysaccharides. The majority of them consist of fiber. In contrast with simple carbs they provide a consistent, slow release of energy into the bloodstream. Complex carbs are nutritionally dense, being packed with vitamins and minerals. Complex carbs include starchy and fibrous vegetables as well as grains. Fiber is essential to efficient bodily function as it provides bulk for the intestinal contents, aids in digestion and the elimination of waste and helps ward of digestive tract disease and colon cancer. In addition, fiber can help you to lose body fat. Because they are so low in calories, you can eat a lot of them without impacting on your calorie count. The smart person, then, will use fibrous carbs to add bulk to their meals so that they aren't eating too many calorie dense starchy carbs and proteins. Eating a starchy carb AND a fibrous carb at each meal will provide an ideal macronutrient mix.

Rather than staying away from carbs all together, the person who is interested in a balanced, sensible fat loss nutritional program will focus on eating natural, unprocessed carbs. She will reduce refined, processed carbs as much as possible. White sugar and white flour products should be on the 'no go' list.

FRUIT FACTS

Fruit provides natural sugars in the form of fructose. Fructose has been blamed as a fat stimulator and many people avoid eating fruit as a result. The fructose myth, however, has been well and truly laid to rest by scientific studies and fruit should be an integral part of any sound nutritional plan. A piece of fruit is a great source of vitamins and minerals as well as carotenoids, flavonoids and polyphenols, all of which promote heart health. Fruits are also high in fiber while being low in total calorie count.

HOW MANY CARBS?

Aim for 50% of your total daily caloric intake from natural carbohydrates. 25 to 35 grams of these carbs should be in the form of fiber. To pack mass onto your frame, you need to be taking in 2 grams of carbohydrate per pound of bodyweight. So, if you weight 180 pounds, you'll need . . .

180 x 2 = 260 grams of carbs per day

Over the course of six meals, this equates to about 44 grams of carbs per meal. In terms of calories, he should eat 1500 calories per day of carbohydrate, mixed between fibrous and starchy varieties. If he is eating six small meals over the course of the day, he will be ingesting approximately 250 carb calories per meal. Use the following lists to plan out the carb component of your meals.

Starchy Carbs:

Potatoes

Sweet Potatoes

Yams

Oats

Beans

Brown Rice

Lentils

Chickpeas

Pumpkin

Quinoa

Millet

Fibrous Carbs:

Broccoli

Spinach

Asparagus

Cucumber

Tomatoes

Cauliflower

Brussels Sprouts

Celery

Onions

Carrots

Mushrooms

FACTOR SIX

DRINK YOUR WATER

Your muscles are 70 percent water. In order to make them bigger, you need to keep them hydrated. If you don't drink enough water, your muscles will shrink. Dehydration causes water to come out of the muscle cell. This puts the body into a catabolic state. That's why it is critical to keep your muscles flushed with water.

It is especially critical to get water into your body first thing in the morning. You've just been in a fasted state during the night. As well as not eating, you haven't been drinking water. That is why you should consume half a liter of water first thing in the morning. And that means actual real, pure water. If you're one of those who need a coffee to wake them up, you might have to rethink that habit. Caffeine is a diuretic. It will take even more water from your system.

If you need a bit of flavor to make your water more palatable, place a slice of lemon in your water jar. Set your sights on a gallon (almost 4 liters) of water per day. You should also drink water while you're working out. Forget about those expensive sports drinks. With your short duration workouts you don't need them. But you do need water.

Carry a water bottle with you at all times and sip from it regularly. Replace sodas and fruit drinks with flavored water. Set you sights on that gallon a day target and, remember that water is just as important to your muscle building efforts as protein is.

FACTOR SEVEN

BOOST YOUR TESTOSTERONE

Testosterone is the male growth hormone that is primarily responsible for muscle growth. It also boosts your sex drive. Clearly, then, you need as much of it as you can get. We produce testosterone in our testes. Most men are capable of producing about 7 mg of testosterone each day. Our testosterone levels peak at about the age of 20. It then declines but not at a marked pace.

Here's what testosterone does to help you get massive and strong:

- Increases lean muscle mass and reduces body fat

- Promotes positive nitrogen balance

- Promotes fat metabolism

- Stimulates red blood cell production, expanding blood volume and improving oxygen delivery throughout the body.

5 WAYS TO BOOST TESTOSTERONE LEVELS

1. Weight train

2. Eliminate cardio

3. Sleep - get a minimum of seven hours

4. Eat more red meat

5. Lean out – the body produces more testosterone when our body fat percentage is under 15 percent.

*This is my favorite resource for raising testosterone to maximum levels, naturally → Natural Testosterone

FACTOR EIGHT

BOOST YOUR GROWTH HORMONE LEVELS

The body naturally produces growth hormone in the pituitary gland and, as its name implies, it is responsible for cell growth and regeneration. Increasing muscle mass and bone density are impossible without human growth hormone. However, it is also a major player in maintaining the health of all human tissue, including that of the brain and other vital organs. The secreted growth hormone remains active in the bloodstream for only a few minutes, but this is enough time for the liver to convert it into growth factors, the most critical of which is insulin-like growth factor-1 or IGF-1. IGF-1 boosts a host of anabolic properties. Scientists began to harvest growth hormone from the pituitary glands of cadavers in the 1950's, but didn't synthesize the first human growth hormone (HGH) in laboratories until 1981, with it's use as a performance enhancing drug becoming popular thereafter.

HGH inhibits insulin, which is the fat storing hormone. Sadly, from about age 21 onward, our bodies start producing less and less HGH. That's why younger people can get away with eating junk food and not pack on the pounds, whereas someone in their 50's only has to look at a pizza to gain weight. Over eating also mucks up our HGH levels. Balancing your HGH levels will not only help you to lose weight, it will but you in an anabolic state to promote muscle growth and keep you looking young and fantastic.

Let's find what you can do – legally and safely – to boost your own HGH levels.

(1)   EAT A BALANCED DIET

Diet is the third major factor in keeping growth hormone levels topped off. It is necessary to eat a balanced diet that provides as many of the following growth hormone boosting agents as possible:

- Vitamin A

- Vitamin B5

- Vitamin B12

- Folic Acid

- Inositol Heaxanicotinate

- Chromium

- Zinc

- Magnesium

- Iodine

- Glutamine

- Glycine

- Carnitine

- Arginine

- Taurine

- Lysine

- Ornithine Alpha-ketoglutarate

(2) WORK OUT WITH WEIGHTS

Lifting heavy weights over a regular period of time releases human growth hormone. By reducing our rest between sets this process is enhanced. Try to keep your between set rest periods to under a minute for the best results. Focus, too, on compound movements that work your major muscles groups together, such as squats, deadlift and bent over rowing. Short bouts on high intensity aerobic exercise performed for bouts of about 10 minutes at a time are also effective for HGH release.

(3) SUPPLEMENT

A multivitamin provides many of the nutrients needed to boost growth hormone. Amino acids such as arginine and glutamine have been shown to boost growth hormone levels in separate studies. Instead of taking these separately, you now have the choice between a multitude of specialty supplements.

Other hormones, such as testosterone, estrogen, progesterone, can also lead to growth hormone increases. The following compounds have all been shown to enhance growth hormone levels;

- Colostrum

- Alpha GPC

- Tribulus terrestris

- Coleus forskohlii

- Panax ginseng

- Siberian ginseng

- Aswagandha root

- Schizandra berry

- Astragalus root

- Dong quai

- Wild yam extract

- Goji berry

- Red date berry

(4) SLEEP

Our natural growth hormone production hits its peak at night time. It is, in fact, part of the vital repair and restoration process of sleep. But the daily surge in HGH production doesn't happen when we're awake. It's vital, then, to establish and maintain a regular sleep pattern.

FACTOR NINE

EAT EVERY THREE WAKING HOURS

The way that the majority of people in the Western world eat is the mirror opposite to the way that they should eat. Which probably explains why we are drowning in the midst of an obesity epidemic. Consider the traditional 3 meals per day that we've all grown up on ...

After six to eight hours of fasting, our bodies need the energy that breakfast promises. However most people don't give their bodies the fuel they need at the start of the day. They either skip breakfast all together, or they shovel heavily processed, sugar-encrusted cereals down their throat. That's usually chased down with coffee – and more sugar.

As a result of these less than ideal breakfast choices, many people get hungry around 10am. Muffin break anyone?

For many people lunch consists of a mix of processed carbohydrates and fat – with a soft drink chaser.

By the time that dinner rolls around, most people are starving. They load their plates to the hilt and then eat like there's no tomorrow. When they finally walk away from the dinner table they are so gorged with calories that all they want to do is sleep – which is exactly what they do. And what happens while they sleep? – all those calories are going straight to their belly!

Today you are going to learn a better way - a way that will not only stop your fat accumulation in it's tracks but that will actually reprogram your body from a fat storage warehouse into a **muscle building super furnace.**

Eat every 3 waking hours: Forget about the traditional 3 meals per day eating plan. It is bad for you. From now on you will eat more often and on a regular schedule. Each meal will be about the same size. As well as preventing binge eating and grazing, eating regularly will allow a constant flow of energy to your system. The very act of digesting your food will also rev up your metabolism

MAKING IT WORK FOR YOU

In order to be able to stick with an eating plan it has to be easy to work with. That means it should be easy to prepare, easy to carry your food with you so that you avoid convenience eating and easy to eat. In order to do that you will prepare your meals ahead of time and store them in Tupperware containers. Every meal will combine protein and carbs. Getting into the habit of prepping your food ahead of time will allow you to have the food ready to eat right when you need it. That, in itself, will go a long way toward helping you to stay consistent with your 80% clean eating diet plan.

Putting your food in Tupperware encourages you to eat the food that you've prepped, making it easy to eat healthy. This system will prevent you from cheating, putting you on the path to automatic consistency. Also, with this system you only have to cook once every 4 or 5 days. That saves you having to wash pots and pans, rush around after work while you're starving and stopping in at McDonald's just to get you through. Prepping your food and putting it in a container will save you between 7 and 14 hours every week.

A key to success with this system is to keep your food choices limited. Stick to just one or two carb and protein sources for the week. If you do this you will be able to prepare your entire food for the week in less than two hours.

HOT FOOD ON THE GO

So you've prepped your meals and put them in Tupperware containers. How are you going to keep them hot when you're out and about? Simple! Buy a small food cooler and a standard hot water bottle. In the morning put your containers in the microwave for 10 minutes. At the same time boil some water and pour it into the hot water bottle. Now put the containers in the cooler and cover them with a towel. Place the hot water bottle in there as well and close the lid. Your meals will stay hot for up to 8 hours!

Chapter Seven

5 SUPER SUPPLEMENTS

The bodybuilding supplement business is a multi-billion dollar industry that, especially over the last decade, has been making a killing. And it's the young (and not so young), eager gym goers desperate to pack muscle onto their frame who have been dying. Unscrupulous companies plaster their promotional material with images or steroid induced behemoths who claim that you have simply got to take their supplement to have any show of building muscle. After a few years of wasted investment, a lot of frustrated hard gainers simply give up.

Yet it needn't be that way. It is possible to wade through the masses of useless junk to find the supplementary gems that will actually help you to pack muscle onto your frame. You simply have to now what you're looking for.

In this chapter we present 5 key muscle building supplements that you should be adding to your nutritional arsenal.

SUPER SUPPLEMENT NO. 1: PROTEIN DRINKS

Protein builds muscle. That's why it's essential that protein forms the basis of your nutritional plan, especially before and immediately after your workout. Getting quality, lean protein into your body in the form of whole foods at these times can be tricky. That's where protein powders come into their own. They're quick, cost effective and they channel their nutrients directly to the muscle cells that are craving them. Taste is another issue entirely. Many powders out there taste like sawdust. That's why we set out to find the best tasting protein powder on the market today. After all, if you don't like it, you won't keep taking it. And, just like with your training, consistency of protein intake is the key to success. Getting hold of the best tasting protein powder will make it easy for you keep up your intake. Here's on overview of what you need to look for when considering your protein powder.

TASTE

Taste, of course, is a subjective thing. We all like different flavors and types of food. When it come to protein powders, however, we can all identify the winners from the losers. Some products on the market, despite announcing a mouthwatering taste on their packaging, are virtually inedible. It pays, then to either check with family and friends to get recommendations on taste before spending your hard earned money on a product you may not be able to stomach. Alternatively, ask for a taste test before buying.

You'll want to buy a protein powder that mixes effortlessly in your shaker bottle, without leaving residue in the bottom of the bottle. Clumpiness is a no-no, as is a chalky taste. Rather, your mixed drink needs to be smooth, like velvet. The best tasting protein powders will offer a range of flavors, providing a world of variety beyond vanilla and chocolate.

QUALITY

You don't want a protein powder that's going to leave you with gastro-intestinal upsets, cramping or flatulence. A quality product will leave you feeling strong and pumped rather than weak and deflated. It will have a yield rate of 70% or more (that's the percentage of the actual product that is protein). The amino acid profile should include both Branch Chain (BCAA) and

Essential (EAA) amino acids. A combination of casein, whey and egg protein will provide a great protein mix.

RESULTS

Unlike most other foods, protein powders have a job to do. If it doesn't help to build muscle mass, lean you out and provide energy, you should stop using it, even if it is one of the best tasting protein powder on the market. Keep a record over the period that you take the powder, carefully noting your strength improvements and muscle mass gains. You should also check with gym buddies before spending your money on what they have found to be the best product to build muscle.

EASE OF USE

The best tasting protein powders must also provide ease of use. It should mix equally well in a blender, a shaker bottle and with nothing more than a spoon. Make sure that the powder doesn't cling to the sides of the mixing cup or give you mouthfuls of clumpy residue. You also don't want a product that makes you feel bloated, especially if you're taking your protein during the workout.

WHEY OR CASEIN

The two basic types of protein that you'll find on the ingredient list are whey and casein. Whey protein is considered fast acting because it is able to break down into amino acids and get into the bloodstream within 15 minutes of entering the body. Whey is a dairy based protein, and should be your protein of choice prior to and immediately after your workout.

Casein protein is digested more slowly. As a result this is a good option prior to bed, as it will provide a slow release of protein throughout your system during the night hours when your body is busy at its replenishing and rebuilding work.

SUPER SUPPLEMENT NO.2: BRANCH CHAIN AMINO ACIDS

Branch Chain Amino Acids (BCAA's) have long been a favorite of bodybuilders and strength athletes, who have used them to increase protein uptake within the muscle cell a well to boost both intra and post workout energy and recovery. Emergency room workers, too, in hospitals know all about BCAA's. They use them to improve healing and recovery time from injury. As a result of their medical and athletic applications, BCAA's have been subject to a huge number of scientific studies. These studies have given the public at large confidence in the efficacy of supplementing with BCAA's. If you're not using BCAA's to support your muscle building efforts them you are missing out on a vital ingredient. The current consensus is that BCAA's act optimally when taken as a drink during the workout.

Branch-Chain Amino Acids (BCAAs), include the amino acids leucine, isoleucine and valine. All three of these are considered essential amino acids because they are not synthesized by the body and must, therefore be supplied by our diet. BCAA's are unique in that they can be oxidized in the muscles for fuel. The other essential amino acids are broken down in the liver. BCAA's, especially leucine, are key stimulators of protein synthesis and protein breakdown. BCAA's can be used as fuel during exercise. They will also prevent the catabolic effects of working out. Post-workout they can enhance muscle building effects.

BENEFITS OF A BCAA SUPPLEMENT

- Increases metabolism

- Decreases appetite

- Prevents the breakdown of muscle tissue

- Decreases perceived workout exertion allowing you train harder and longer

Recommendations: Most experts recommend a slightly higher dosage of leucine and smaller dosages of valine and isoleucine. Supplement with 8g of BCAAs daily in a ratio of leucine / valine isoleucine of 3:1:1

SUPER SUPPLEMENT NO. 3: GLUTAMINE

Glutamine is the most abundant amino acid found in the human body. It is mainly synthesized and stored in muscles. Heavy weight training is associated with drops in blood glutamine levels, increasing susceptibility to infection. As well as providing athletes with immune support, glutamine supplementation promotes protein synthesis and help prevent muscle breakdown. Glutamine can be especially helpful to trainers who are experiencing burn-out or overtraining.

Recommendation: Glutamine is available in tablet, capsule and powder form. It should be taken pre (30 minutes prior to the workout), during and post workout at a dosage of 4g.

SUPER SUPPLEMENT NO. 4: CREATINE

Creatine is the number one, most popular supplement used by people the world over to gain muscle mass and strength. Several hundred studies have conclusively shown that it does, indeed, improve performance and increase muscle mass.

WHY TAKE CREATINE

Creatine is not a steroid or a drug. In fact, creatine is naturally found in your body. The human body synthesises one gram of creatine per day. So what does creatine do?

Creatine is necessary to produce the energy for high intensity activity, especially those activities that typically last for less then ten seconds – like a weight training repetition. Supplementing with creatine increases your muscular stores of creatine phosphate. Creatine phosphate is necessary to help resynthesize ATP. ATP is what your body needs to lift heavy weight. Studies have shown that creatine will help you to recover from high intensity activity. If you're looking to add some size, creatine will help you to add two to five pounds of lean muscle to your frame.

You can naturally find creatine in meat. However, in order to get one gram of creatine you have to eat about one kilogram of meat. To get the recommended daily amount for muscle gain, you would have to consume 5 kg of meat per day! Supplementing with creatine is a whole lot healthier – and cheaper!

To notice results, you'll want to take 3-5 grams od creatine daily, even on non-workout days. Studies show that it doesn't matter what time of day you take your creatine. They key is to simply keep taking it.

WHAT TO LOOK FOR

There are a huge number of options when you start shopping for creatine. Your first point of reference should be to go for a product that has a base of creatine monohydrate. Monohydrate is the original creatine and it is the one that has been the basis of the majority of creatine studies. It has been proven time and again to enhance the ATP system for increased energy, strength and mass gains. There have been a lot of new creatine variants come along, such as kre-alkyline, which is a 98% monohydrate with a buffer. Creatine hydrochloride requires a lesser amount of creatine, but it is also not as effective as straight monohydrate.

When looking for brands of monohydrate, check the label for Creapure, which is the brand name of a German manufacturer of monohydrate. Creapure have a patented process for how they derive their creatine monohydrate. Choosing Creapure will ensure that you are getting the purest form of creatine monohydrate available.

HOW MUCH DOES IT COST?

When you consider how effective it is, creatine is extremely cheap. You only require 3-5 grams per day. You should expect top pay about four cents per gram. Creatine is available as a powder, a liquid or a capsule. The powder will always be the cheapest, with the liquid being the most expensive, sometimes pushing the per gram cost up to twenty five cents.

SUPER SUPPLEMENT NO. 5: NITRIC OXIDE

You work hard in the gym – and out. You discipline yourself to keep your diet clean and you get the rest and recuperation required to allow your body to grow and respond. You're constantly looking for any advantage that will help you to maximise your workouts and get you to your physique and fitness goals faster. If this sound like you, then Nitric Oxide boosters are a supplement that you definitely need to get familiar with. Let's consider the benefits – and the dangers!

Nitric Oxide is a gas produced by the body. Nitric Oxide boosters are supplements designed to enhance the body's ability to produce nitric oxide. They do this by facilitating the breakdown of the amino acid arginine.

The enhanced level of Nitric oxide in the body then works by promoting more efficient blood delivery to the muscle cells. They do this by widening or dilating blood vessels. This not only encourages better muscle pumps during and after your workouts but also helps to more rapidly transport nutrients to the muscle. This allows you to lift heavier for longer and recover faster from your workouts.

NITRIC OXIDE BENEFITS

The amino acids arginine, citrulline and beta-alanine are the most common ingredients in nitric oxide boosters. These aminos have proven nitric oxide boosting properties. Whether you're looking to build strength, add muscle or recover faster from your workouts, nitric oxide booster supplements will get you there faster. Here are 5 reasons why you should consider nitric oxide supplementation:

Quicker Workout Recovery: By enlarging the blood vessels, NO boosters assist smooth muscle to relax and quicken oxygen delivery to the muscle cell. This along, with the enhanced blood flow will greatly boost your recovery ability.

Less Fatigue While Training: When you're training hard, especially if performing high rep workouts, fatigue can be a major limiting factor. High rep training requires endurance and a limiting factor to endurance performance is oxygen delivery to the muscle tissue. NO boosters have the ability to dramatically improve your oxygen uptake.

More Energy: Improved blood supply to the muscle cell results in a more stable core body temperature. This means that less energy will be required to bring the body's temperature down during hard training. That means that more energy will be available for the workout.

Burns Body Fat: The NO precursor L-arginine increases glucose uptake in the body. It also boosts the body's ability to burn body fat as fuel.

A Great Pump: The increased blood flow to the muscle cell will give an awesome pump to your muscles. You'll look great and feel even better. The pump may not last, but the motivation will.

NITRIC OXIDE SIDE EFFECTS

The muscle, energy and pump inducing benefits of NO Boosters are real and demonstrable. But so are a number of concerning side effects. Here are the key side effects of NO supplementation:

Dizziness and Faint Feeling: NO boosters can drop your blood pressure to abnormal levels, leading to an uneasy, spacy feeling along with light-headedness. This is due to their ability to open up the veins to allow for better oxygen uptake.

Vasodilation and Bleeding. Vasodilation refers to the enhanced ability of the blood vessels to open and relax. NO supplementation will boost this ability with the resultant benefits mentioned above. But there is a downside to increased vasodilation. It can result in low blood pressure and excessive bleeding.

Herpes Susceptibility: The main amino acid in NO supplements is L-Arginine. It just so happens that this amino acid also aggravates the herpes virus. It is not uncommon for a person starting on NO booster supplementation to contract the herpes virus.

Diarrhea, Weakness, Nausea: Overdosing on NO Boosters may lead to these unpleasant effects, primarily as a result of too much L-Arginine.

More Frequent Urination: The higher levels of arginine lead to more frequent urination, both during the day and the night.

Lowered Dopamine Levels: Dopamine is responsible for our levels of motivation, our sleep patterns, cognitive ability and memory. Enhanced nitric oxide uptake, however, has been shown to reduce dopamine production by up to 66%.

Gastrointestinal Problems: Quite a common effect of NO supplementation is bloating, abdominal pain and flatulence. This is mainly due to the high levels of arginine present in most NO products.

REDUCING THE SIDE-EFFECTS

To minimise the effects mentioned above, keep your Arginine levels below 5000 mg per day. Exercise regularly to naturally enhance dopamine levels. The amino acid tyrosine can also boost dopamine levels. Start with small dosages of NO supplements and then build up to the daily recommended levels. You can also divide your supplementation intake throughout the day. Don't take nitric oxide if you suffer from hypotension.

SHOULD I OR SHOULDN'T I?

Whether to take nitric oxide supplements is a choice that must be individually weighed. Many people take them with no apparent adverse reactions while others may notice the majority of the above listed side effects within a day or two. If you feel that the benefits outweigh the potential risks, experiment with NO boosters for a six week period, carefully noting the positive and the negative results that you experience. If they get you bigger, stronger and more pumped without apparent harm, you've just found a winner. If not, you'll know not to go there again. Either way, you will have benefited.

Chapter Eight

TOP 10 MUSCLE BUILDING SHAKE RECIPES

Getting your protein in the form of a delicious, healthy shake seems like the ideal muscle nutrition solution. It can be, but it can also be an expensive trap for the unwary. The number of protein and muscle gain powder options out there is mind boggling. Unfortunately, many of them are loaded with fillers, artificial sweeteners and low grade quality sources that will clog up your system and make you fat. When it comes to buying protein powder, it is definitely a case of *caveat emptor* –let the buyer beware!

When it comes to protein supplement drinks, there are actually two different kinds that you need to be aware of. Firstly there re protein drinks that have no added calories except for those found in the protein itself. These will typically give you a total calorie count of about 150 calories. On the other hand, there are weight gainer dinks that are packed with extra calories in addition to what is contained in the protein. These may give you as mush as 2000 calories in a single serving!

The following ten muscle building shake recipes will give you a constant source of variety as you mix up delicious muscle building meals in an instant that will satisfy both your taste buds and your muscle cells.

BERRY SMOOTHIE

- 3 oz mixed berries

- 2 tsp maple syrup

- 2 tbs orange juice

- 1 medium banana, frozen

- 2 tbs protein powder

- 12 cup cold mineral water

Remove the stems from the berries and place them in the blender. Add the maple syrup and orange juice and blend thoroughly for 15 seconds. Cut the frozen banana into several pieces. Add the banana, protein powder and water to the blender and blend for 15 seconds.

Pour the mixture into a frosted cocktail glass and serve with a straw.

Berries are jam packed with vitamins and minerals. They fill you with energy, calm the nerves and leave you feeling fit and healthy.

MANGO AND COCONUT SMOOTHIE

- 1 piece mango

- 1 lime

- 2 tsp brown sugar

- ¼ cup cold unsweetened coconut milk

- 2 tbs protein powder

- ½ cup cold unfiltered apple juice

- 1-2 tbs grated coconut

Remove a spiral shaped strip of zest from the lime and set it aside. Squeeze out the lime juice, then add the lime juice, sugar and coconut milk to the blender. Blend vigorously for 15 seconds.

Add the protein powder and apple juice. Blend thoroughly for an additional 10 seconds.

Moisten the rim of a large glass with water, turn the glass upside down and dip the rim into the grated coconut. Place ice cubes in the glass and place the blended smoothie over the top. Thread the reserved mango cubes onto a cocktail skewer and lay them across the rim of the glass. Garnish with lime juice and serve with a zest of lime.

STRAWBERRRY PINEAPPLE MIX

- 3 oz strawberries

- 2 tsp lemon juice

- 1 tsp floral honey

- 2/3 cup cold pineapple juice

- 2 tbs protein powder

Wash the berries and set aside one large berry for garnish. Remove the stems from the remaining berries and cut them into quarters. Put the strawberries, lemon juice, honey and half the pineapple juice in a blender and blend thoroughly for 15 seconds.

Add the protein powder and remaining juice and blend for an additional 10 seconds. Pour the mixture into a tall glass. Cut partway into the reserved strawberry and place it on the rim of the glass for garnish. Serve with a straw.

KIWI AVOCADO MIX

- 2 oz ripe avocado

- 1 kiwifruit

- 2 tbs lemon juice

- 1 tsp brown sugar

- ½ cup cold mineral water

- 2 tsp protein powder

- 1 sprig fresh mint

Peel the avocado and chop the flesh, removing the pip. Put the avocado in a blender and drizzle with the lemon juice. Set aside one nice kiwifruit slice for garnish. Peel the remaining kiwifruit, chop it coarsely and add it to the blender along with the sugar and half the mineral water. Blend thoroughly for 15 seconds. Add the protein powder and remaining mineral water and blend thoroughly for an additional 10 seconds.

Place ice cubes in a large glass and pour avocado mixture over the top. Cut partway into the reserved kiwi slice and place on the rim of the glass. Garnish with the mint.

APPLE ELDEBERRY SMOOTHIE

- 3 oz tart apple

- 2 tsp lemon juice

- 2 tsp floral honey

- 2/3 cup cold, unfiltered apple juice

- 2 tbs protein powder

- ¼ cup cold elderberry juice

- 1 sprig fresh mint

Wash the apple and set aside a nice wedge for garnish. Peel the remaining apple, remove the core, and cut into small pieces. Place in the blender and blend for 15 seconds.

Add the protein powder and elderberry juice and blend for a further 10 seconds. Place ice cubes in a large glass and pour the mixture over them. Put the apple wedge on the rim of the glass. Garnish with mint and serve with a straw.

ALMOND ATTACKER

- 1 cup almond milk

- 2 scoops protein powder (soy based)

- ½ cup oatmeal

- 2 tablespoons dark chocolate

Put all these ingredients in a blender and blitz.

Almonds are full of healthy fats that help mental alertness. Optimum brain power equals optimum body power. This drink is ideal for people with stomach sensitivity, as there are no dairy products in this smoothie, its ideal for those who suffer from lactose intolerance. Oatmeal has a low GI, making it slow burning, leaving you feel fuller for longer. Dark chocolate is an anti-oxidant, helping kill off any free radicals in your system.

BANANARAMA

- 1 frozen banana

- 1 cup skim milk

- 1 tablespoon cinnamon

- 1 scoop protein powder

- ½ cup desiccated coconut

Put all these ingredients in a blender and blitz

Bananas are full of potassium, which promotes heart and kidney vitality. Cinnamon helps blood circulation and good blood circulation helps stimulate weight loss.

CHOCOLATE PEAR SHAKE

- 2/3 cups low fat milk

- 4 oz ripe pear

- 1 tsp orange juice

- 1 tsp orange juice concentrate

- 2 tbs finely grated chocolate

- 2 tsp protein powder

Heat the milk until lukewarm. Wash the pear, setting aside a nice piece for garnish. Peel the remaining pear, remove the core, and cut into pieces than place in the blender. Add the orange juice, apple juice and chocolate (leaving a little aside for garnish) and half of the milk. Blend thoroughly for fifteen seconds.

Add the protein powder and remaining milk and blend for a further 10 seconds. Pour the mixture into a tall glass and place the pear slice on the rim. Sprinkle with the remaining chocolate and serve with a straw.

CHERRY BUTTERMILK SMOOTHIE

- 4 oz sweet cherries

- 1 sprig fresh mint

- 1 tbs lemon juice

- 2 tsp apple juice concentrate

- 2 tsp protein powder

- 2/3 cup cold buttermilk

Wash the cherries and set aside a pair joined by the stem for garnish. Remain the pits from the remaining cherries and place the cherries in the blender. Remove the leaves from the mint and set aside one or two nice leaves. Chop the remaining mint leaves and add them to the blender along with the lemon juice, apple juice concentrate, protein powder and half of the buttermilk. Blend thoroughly for fifteen seconds.

Add the remaining buttermilk and blend for a further 10 seconds. Pour into a tall glass, hanging the reserved cherries over the rim and garnishing with the reserved mint leaves.

MANGO CARROT MIX

- 1 piece mango

- 1 tbs lime juice

- 2 tsp floral honey

- 2/3 cup cold carrot juice

- 2 tbs protein powder

- 2 pinches ground ginger

- 2 carrot strips

Peel the mango. Cut a wedge and aside a piece for garnishing. Coarsely chop the remaining mango and place in the blender. Add the lime juice, honey and half the carrot juice and blend for fifteen seconds.

Add the remaining carrot juice, ginger and protein powder and blend for a further 10 seconds. Place ice cubes in a large glass and pour the mixture over them. Garnish with the reserved mango wedge. Place the carrot strips on the rim of the glass.

Chapter Nine

BRINGING IT ALL TOGETHER

You now have the blueprint for building the new you. Follow the advice in this book over the next 12 months and you WILL pack between 8 and 20 solid pounds of muscle mass onto your body. If that doesn't sound like much to you, go out and grab hold of a pound of lean steak. Now, imagine a dozen or so of those cuts of prime beef slapped all over your physique. Believe me, that will make a dramatic difference to the way that you look!

As you travel along your journey to a more massive physique, you will encounter all sorts of well meaning people who will offer you advice, frown at what you're doing and try to sell you on the latest sure thing. Your job, however, is to stay focused on the two workout phases that will be your training life over the next 12 months. Too many people get started on a good thing and then switch to something else before giving it time to work. Don't be one of them.

WHERE TO FROM HERE?

Reclaiming your body, grasping hold of your physical destiny and forging the body that you desire is about more than knowledge.

It's about action.

This book has given you the knowledge. In fact it has provided a template of exactly what you need to do – and avoid – in order to sculpt the physique of your dreams, despite your genetic limitations. The question is . . .

What are you going to do with that knowledge?

Are you going to be like the 70% of people who purchase exercise and nutrition guides and do . . .

Nothing?

Are you going to apply the clear direction we've provided on nutrition, and proper, scientific training **OR** are you going to continue spinning your wheels, flitting from one unproductive training regimen to another with nothing to show for it?

Are you going to take the workout challenge, forget the archaic nonsense about genetic limitations, and use the iron to shape and transform your physique **OR** are you going slip back onto the couch and resume the go nowhere lifestyle which has shaped the physique that you now possess?

Are you going to transform your mental landscape, energising it with the power of goal setting and positive thinking to catapult you forward like an unstoppable cyborg **OR** are you going to languish in a world of stinking thinking, convincing yourself that you are unable to build muscle, get in shape and make traction in your life?

The choice is yours.

Make the right one.

BONUS - Anabolic Recipes

took these recipes straight from my absolute favorite muscle building cook book. It's from my good friend Dave Ruel's Anabolic Cooking Cookbook:

==> Dave Ruel's Anabolic Cooking Cookbook

The cool thing about this recipe is that you can make it at different times during the day:

- For Breakfast
- Pre-Workout, about an hour before you hit the gym
- Post-workout

Try it, I'm about 110% sure you'll like it!

Talk to you soon ,

Augustus Sims

PS: Dave Ruel's Cookbook features over 200 "Anabolicious" step-by-step, easy to make recipes, so you will never be bored with your diet again. You will become a chef in no time, and will keep your family and friends healthy along the way.

Dave shows you how to cook tasty meals for your muscle building and fitness goals no matter what they may be. You will learn every aspect of cooking for healthy living and reaching physique goals.

And it's more than just a cookbook, "Anabolic Cooking" is a complete nutrition guide full of Cooking tricks, Nutritional Tips and Dieting Strategies...

Make sure to go grab your copy: Dave Ruel's Anabolic Cooking Cookbook

Check Out Some of the Recipes Just Ahead...

BREAKFAST

Dave Ruel's Anabolic Blueberry Oatmeal

*Makes 1 Serving

Ingredients
- 3/4 cup oatmeal
- 8 Egg Whites
- 1/2 scoop (15g) of Chocolate Protein Powder
- 2 teaspoons of Pure Cocoa Powder
- 1 teaspoon of Splenda
- 1 tbsp of Flax Oil
- 1 cup of frozen Blueberries
- 1/4 cup of water

Directions
1. In a big bowl, mix All the ingredients (except for the frozen blueberries)

2. Cook in a microwave for about 3-4 minutes (cooking time vary from one microwave to the other) - stir the mix 2 minutes after cooking has started (so the mix doesn't stick or create chunks)

3. Once the mix is cooked, add the frozen blueberries, mix everything and enjoy :)

Nutritional Facts (Per Serving)

Calories: 580

Protein: 52g

Carbohydrates: 57g

Fat: 16g

HIGH PROTEIN PANCAKES

Makes 1 Serving (6 pancakes)

Ingredients
- 1/4 cup oatmeal

- 6 egg whites

- 1 tbsp ground flax

- 1/2 tbsp cinnamon

- 1/4 teaspoon of Baking Soda

- 1 teaspoon of Splenda

Directions

1. First heat a frying pan until hot and then reduce to medium temperature.

2. After mixing together all the ingredients in a blender, spray some pam (or other cooking spray), drop by spoonful onto the plan, flipping when bubbles start to form.

3. Make about 6 pancakes.

Nutritional Facts

(Per Serving)

Calories: 259

Protein: 30g

Carbohydrates: 26g

Fat: 4g

CHICKEN & POULTRY RECIPES

Dave's Famous Turkey Meat Loaf

Makes 6 Servings

Ingredients

- 2 lbs of ground Turkey

- 1 teaspoon of olive oil

- 1 diced Onion

- 1 teaspoon of Garlic(optional)

- 1/3 cup Dried Tomatoes

- 1 cup of Whole Wheat Bread Crumbs

- 1 Whole Eggs

- 1/2 cup of Parsley

- 1/4 cup of Low Fat Parmesan

- 1/4 cup Skim Milk

- Salt and Pepper

- 1 teaspoon of Oregano

Directions

1. Cook the Onion with Olive Oil separatly

2. Mix everything together in a big bowl, add the cooked oignons

3. Put the mix in a big pan

4. Bake at 375-400 F for about 30mins

Nutritional Facts

(Per Serving)

Calories: 393

Protein: 46g

Carbohydrates: 14g

Fat: 17g

BAKED CRISPY CHICKEN NUGGETS

Makes 6 Servings

Ingredients

- 3 boneless, skinless chicken breasts weighing about 6 oz. / 170 g each
- 1/4 cup / 60 ml of oat bran
- 1/4 cup / 60 ml of wheat germ
- 1 Tbsp / 15 ml coarsely ground flaxseed
- 1/4 cup / 60 ml coarsely ground almonds
- 1/2 tsp / 2 1/2 ml sea salt
- 1/2 tsp / 2 1/2 ml white pepper
- Pinch garlic powder
- 1/2 cup / 120 ml water or low-sodium chicken broth
- 1 large egg white, lightly beaten

Directions

1. Preheat oven to 400°F. Prepare baking sheet by lining with parchment paper or coating lightly with best-quality olive oil.

2. Cut chicken breasts into nugget-sized pieces, about 1.5 inches square. Set aside.

3. Next, combine all dry ingredients in a large container with a tightly fitting lid. Shake well. This is your coating mixture.

4. Combine water and egg in a medium bowl. Dip each piece in the water/egg-white mixture. Then dip each piece in the coating mixture. Make sure each piece is well coated.

5. Place on the baking sheet. When all of your chicken has been coated and your baking sheet is full, place in the oven and bake for 10-15 minutes or until golden.

Nutritional Facts

(Per Serving - 4 Nuggets)
Calories: 100
Protein: 12g
Carbohydrates: 7g
Fat: 3.5g

RED MEAT & PORK RECIPES

The Muscle Cook's chili

Makes 9 Servings

Ingredients
1.5 lbs Ground Buffalo (Bison) or Extra Lean Ground Beef
1 cup diced Onions
1 diced Green Pepper
Garlic (3 cloves, minced)

1 tbsp Chili Powder

1 teaspoon Turmeric

1 teaspoon Oregano

2 Cans (15oz/can) Black Beans

2 Cans (15oz/can) Diced Tomatoes (with juice)

1 Can (14oz) Low Sodium Beef Broth

1/4 teaspoon salt / 1 teaspoon Pepper

Directions

1. In a pan, Cook the Buffalo, Green Pepper, Onions, Garlic for 5-6 mins, until it is almost cooked.

2. Transfer everything in a big casserole. Add Chili powder, Turmeric, Oregano, Beans, Tomatoes, Broth, salt and pepper.
3. Make it boil
4. Reduce intensity and stir for 20 mins
until it reaches wanted thickness

Nutritional Facts
(Per Serving - 1 cup)

Calories: 264

Protein: 30g

Carbohydrates: 26g

Fat: 4.5g

BUFFALO (BISON) BURGERS
Makes 4 Servings

Ingredients
- 1 Tbsp od olive oil

- 1 chopped onion

- 2 egg whites

- 1/4 cup oat bran

- 1/4 cup cooked, mashed sweet potato

- 1 teaspoon oregano

- 1/2 teaspoon sea salt

- 1/2 teaspoon ground black pepper

- 1 lb / 455 g ground bison

Directions

1. Heat olive oil over medium heat in a skillet. Cook the onion until soft and golden. Set aside.

2. Meanwhile, in a large bowl, mix together egg whites, oat bran, sweet potato, oregano, sea salt and pepper.

3. Stir in onions and bison. Mix the ingredients together with clean hands until just combined. Take a handful of the meat and create 4 flat patties.

4. Grill the patties on each side until the burgers reach desired doneness.

Nutritional Facts

(Per Serving - 1 x 4oz Patty)

Calories: 143

Protein: 22g

Carbohydrates: 6g

Fat: 2g

FISH & SEAFOOD

Citrus Baked Tilapia

Makes 4 Servings

Ingredients
* - 1 pound fresh tilapia fillets
* - 2 Tbsp. extra virgin olive oil
* - 1 Tbsp. lime zest
* - 1/4 cup freshly-squeezed lime juice
* - 1/4 cup orange juice (preferably freshly-squeezed)
* - 1/2 thai red pepper (optional, only if you like it spicy)
* - 1 tsp. seasalt
* - 1/2 tsp. freshly-ground black pepper

Directions
* 1. In a bowl, mix olive oil, lime zest, lime juice, orange juice, chili sauce and salt and pepper.
* 2. Place tilapia fillets in the dish, turning to coat well with marinade.
* 3. Bake 10 to 12 minutes at 400 degrees F or until the fish flakes easily with a fork.

Nutritional Facts
(Per Serving)
Calories: 193
Protein: 33g

Carbohydrates: 0g

Fat: 9g

CLASSIC TUNA MELT PATTIES
Makes 2 Servings

Ingredients

- 16oz. can tuna, drained

- 1 egg white, beaten

- 2 tablespoon of oatmeal

- 2 tablespoon of onion, diced (or 1/4 teaspoon of onion powder)

- 1/4 teaspoon garlic powder

- salt & pepper

Directions

1. Mix all ingredients except cheese together in a small bowl

2. Heat a small non-stick frying pan over medium heat and spray with non-stick cooking spray

3. Make two small patties and cook until both sides are brown

Nutritional Facts
(Per Serving)

Calories: 144

Protein: 25g

Carbohydrates: 4g

Fat: 2g

SNACKS & BARS RECIPES

Banana Maple Protein Snack Wraps

Makes 1 Serving

Ingredients
- 1 8" 100% Whole Wheat Wrap
- 1 medium banana
- 1 tablespoons of all natural peanut butter (or almond butter)
- 1 tablespoon of slivered almonds
- 1 scoop of vanilla protein powder
- 1 tablespoons of sugar free maple syrup

Directions
1. In a separate bowl, mash banana and protein powder together with a fork until combined.
2. Spread the peanut butter onto the tortilla. Top with the banana mixture.
3. Sprinkle with almonds, then drizzle with maple syrup.
4. Roll the wrap and enjoy!

Nutritional Facts
(Per Serving - 1 Wrap)
Calories: 479
Protein: 33g
Carbohydrates: 52g
Fat: 15g

HIGH PROTEIN FUDGE BARS

Makes 5 Bars

Ingredients
- 8 scoops chocolate protein powder
- 1 cup oatmeal
- 1/3 cup natural peanut butter
- 3 tbsp honey
- 1/2 cup 1% milk
- 3 tbsp crushed peanuts

Directions
1. Mix together the protein powder, oatmeal, peanut butter, honey and milk.
2. Form into 5 bars and then roll in the crushed peanuts to finish.
3. Place in the fridge for about 30 mins

Nutritional Facts
(Per Serving - 1 Bar)
Calories: 452
Protein: 50g
Carbohydrates: 36g
Fat: 12g

STRAWBERRY MERINGUES

Makes 2 Servings

Ingredients

- 6 egg whites
- 1/4 tsp cream of tartar
- 2 cups sliced strawberries
- 2 tbsp Splenda
- 4 scoops vanilla or strawberry protein powder

Directions

1. Preheat the oven to 250 degrees F.

2. In a large mixing bowl, beat 6 egg whites and 1/4 tsp of cream of tartar with an electric mixer on medium-high speed, until the egg whites become fluffy and hold stiff peaks.

3. Scoop this mixture out into two large ball-like portions on a baking sheet lined with parchment paper.

4. With the back of a large spoon, depress the middle of each portion to form a pocket (this is where the fruit will go).

5. Bake in the oven until the mixture turns light golden brown, between 5 and 10 minutes. Remove from oven and set aside to let cool.

6. Cut up 2 cups of strawberries and mix in a bowl with Splenda. Add the protein powder to this mixture, 1 scoop at a time, mixing well. Once these dry ingredients are mixed together, add water – 1 tbsp at a time – until the mixture becomes creamy.

7. Pour the strawberry mixture into the meringue pockets, letting it flow over the sides. Serve cool.

Nutritional Facts
(Per Serving)
Calories: 330
Protein: 52g

Carbohydrates: 20g

Fat: 4g

SHAKES RECIPES

Banana Bread Shake

Makes 1 Shake

Ingredients
- 2 scoops Vanilla Whey Protein
- 1 Banana
- 1/2 Cup Quaker Oatmeal (cooked in water)
- 1/2 Cup Bran Flakes
- 350ml of Water
- 30g of Dextrose (Only if consumed Post-Workout)

Directions

Blend and Enjoy!

Nutritional Facts
Calories: 498

Protein: 56g

Carbohydrates: 64g (34g if no Dextrose)

Fat: 2g

MUSCLEBERRY BLAST SHAKE

Makes 1 Shake

Ingredients

- 2 scoops Vanilla Whey Protein
- 1.5 Cup of Frozen Berries Mix (Strawberries. Raspberries, Blueberries, Blackberries…)
- 4 Tablespoons of fat-Free Yogurt
- 200ml of Water
- 25g of Dextrose (Only if consumed Post-Workout)

Directions

Blend and Enjoy!

Nutritional Facts

Calories: 380

Protein: 54g

Carbohydrates: 51g (26g if no Dextrose)

Fat: 0g

I'd highly recommend you get the remainder of this cookbook for just a few bucks below:

Dave Ruel's Anabolic Cooking Cookbook

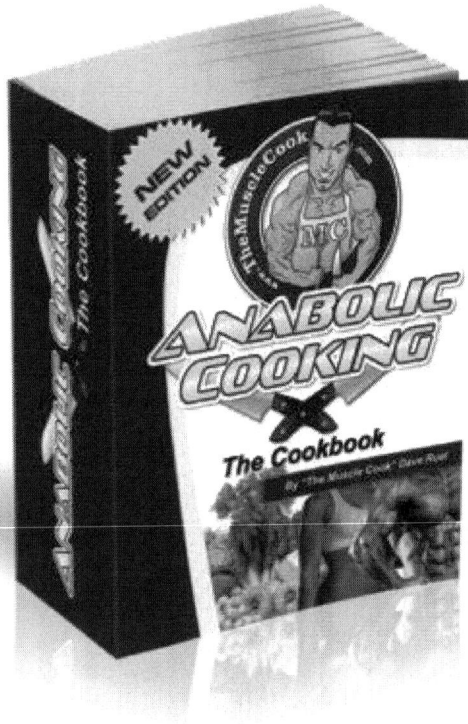

I'd love to hear about your progress. Stay in touch and update me on how things are going at agustusmuscle@gmail.com

Conclusion

Thank you again for downloading this book.

If you enjoyed this book, then I'd like to ask you for a favor, would you be kind enough to leave a review for this book on Amazon? It'd be greatly appreciated!

Help us better serve you by sending questions or comments to augustusmuscle@gmail.com

Printed in Great Britain
by Amazon.co.uk, Ltd.,
Marston Gate.